THE BEST OF
Dierbergs

THE BEST OF
Dierbergs

Treasured Recipes
to Share
with Family & Friends

ACKNOWLEDGMENTS

A special thank you to the Dierbergs family for their vision and support of the Consumer Affairs Department. And to Dierbergs staff home economists, who have, for twenty-five years, contributed culinary expertise and creativity to create a collection of recipes that has been thoroughly tested and loved by customers.

Director of Marketing and Advertising
John Muckerman

Editor
Barb Ridenhour

Cookbook Project Manager
Janice Martin

Copywriters
Gena Bast, Therese Lewis

Consulting Art Director
Mike Parker

Dierbergs School of Cooking Managers
Loretta Evans, Jennifer Kassel, Nancy Lorenz, Pam Pahl

Photographer
Steve Adams, Steve Adams Studio

Food Stylist
Ann Schulz

Prop Stylist, Dierbergs Test Kitchen Manager
Karen Hurych

Nutrition Analysis
Trish Tolbert, D.T.R., Dierbergs;
Sherri Hoyt, R.D., Claudia Humphrey, R.D., Missouri Baptist Medical Center

Missouri Baptist
Medical Center
BJC HealthCare™

Proofreading/Recipe Editing
Patty Tomaselli

Contributors
Linda Behrends, Cathy Chipley, Lorene Greer, Denise Hall, Jeannie Rader

Junior Chef
Abby Ridenhour

TABLE OF CONTENTS

The Robert J. Dierberg Family   *From left to right: Greg and Susan Dierberg, Brian Dierberg, Sharon and Bob Dierberg, Laura and Dr. Jeff Padousis.*

PREFACE

Ever since I can remember, my life has focused on food. It began even before I was born with a legacy built by my grandfather, William Dierberg. It was in 1914 that he bought the general store where he was employed. The 10-Mile House on Olive Street Road was the first site of a Dierbergs store, and where my history in the food industry began. Most likely, my grandfather never envisioned the impact his business venture would have on me and on future generations of our family.

After growing up in the family business, the importance of making food preparation an enjoyable task became a driving force in the contemporary Dierbergs philosophy. And that's why I see Dierbergs striving to be not only a state-of-the-art grocer, offering the best and freshest foods, but also a consumer educator, teaching our customers the newest and best ways to prepare home-cooked meals.

In 1978, Dierbergs opened the first in-store cooking school in an American supermarket. Now, with a total of four in-store schools and seven full-time home economists, Dierbergs teaches and entertains more than 20,000 students each year. Our food professionals, very much in tune with our customers and the latest nutrition and food trends, offer our customers a well-rounded wealth of knowledge about wholesome, nutritious family meals and entertaining at home. Time spent in the kitchen is fun, creative and filled with many incredible benefits, one of which is promoting that a delicious meal can bring a family together.

When our family is together, my wife, Sharon, and I will often sit back and observe everyone around the table, gathered from near and far, all talking, laughing, sharing stories and experiences. All the while, our grandchildren are either chasing each other around the table, or hiding under it, squealing with laughter and fun. It sounds like chaos, but we love it!

Yes, the secret to good cooking may begin in the supermarket, but it certainly ends at home, at a table filled with great food, surrounded by family and friends, making memories to be passed to generations yet to come.

I hope you enjoy this book,

Bob Dierberg

Bob Dierberg

The secret to good cooking may begin in the supermarket, but it certainly ends at home, at a table filled with great food, surrounded by family and friends, making memories to be passed to generations yet to come.

INTRODUCTION

We've included something for everyone, and a recipe for every occasion—tasty and tantalizing, fabulous and full of flavor... everything from appetizers to desserts.

Great meals begin at Dierbergs, where you'll find inspiration from a store full of endless choices. Our mission is to unlock the mystery of well-prepared food and encourage your enjoyment of cooking at home. Julia Child said it best: "Some people like to paint pictures, or do gardening, or build a boat in the basement. Other people get a tremendous pleasure out of the kitchen, because cooking is just as creative and imaginative an activity as drawing, or wood carving, or music."

This cookbook has been coming to fruition for many years. With more than twenty-five years of dedication to consumer education, Dierbergs' staff of home economists has quite a recipe collection—from in-store recipe cards, cooking classes, in-store demos, *Dierbergs Recipe Box* TV collection, *Everybody Cooks®* magazines—so many resources!

It is our customers who have encouraged us to create cookbooks. *Dierbergs Everybody Cooks Interactive Cookbook®* on CD, a compilation of recipes from fifteen years of *Everybody Cooks®* magazines, was widely successful. It was inevitable that a printed cookbook had to be.

And so began our adventure. As you can imagine, narrowing down our customers' favorite recipes was quite a challenge. Through the years, we have received positive feedback and numerous recipe success stories. As time goes by, the category of customer "favorites" continues to build—recipes that have become staples prepared for family and friends, recipes that have stood the test of time, some of the most well-savored results of creativity in the kitchen.

We've included something for everyone, and a recipe for every occasion—tasty and tantalizing, fabulous and full of flavor . . . everything from appetizers to desserts. There is an entire chapter devoted to junior chefs, who always enjoy experimenting in the kitchen. To quote Bob Dierberg's wife, Sharon, encouraging their daughter, Laura, when a beginner in the kitchen, "If you can read, you can cook!"

This is a book full of recipes cherished by those at Dierbergs who we consider our best friends—our customers. Our sincerest hope is that you truly enjoy using this cookbook, and that it will become one of the most treasured tools in your kitchen.

DIERBERGS SCHOOL OF COOKING

NUTRITION INFORMATION

Dierbergs Markets, along with Missouri Baptist Medical Center, a member of BJC HealthCare, proudly sponsor Eat Hearty®, an informational program aimed at helping you choose a heart-healthy eating plan. In *The Best of Dierbergs*, you'll find heart-healthy recipes identified by the red heart logo 🍃 shown with the nutrition analysis.

All nutrition information was calculated using Nutritionist Pro, a nutrition analysis program developed by First DataBank, Inc., for The Hearst Corporation.

Criteria Used for Calculating Nutrition Information

- Wherever a choice is given, the following are used: the first ingredient; the lesser amount of an ingredient; the larger number of servings.
- Ingredients without specific amounts listed, such as "optional" or "toppings," have not been included in the analysis. However, when the ingredient is important to the overall success of the recipe, a portion has been calculated. For example, where ingredients call for "sliced French bread," a representative amount is included in the analysis.

Ingredients Used in Nutrition Calculations

- Certain ingredients are considered "standard" for nutrition analysis. They include large eggs, 2% milk, lean ground beef and canned broth. Other ingredient selections were based on information from the USDA and/or readily available brands.
- If a recipe specifies reduced-fat/reduced-sodium products in the ingredient list, these products were used for nutrition analysis.
- Some recipes meet Eat Hearty criteria without modification. You may wish to make additional substitutions to further reduce the fat/sodium content of the recipe.
- Some recipes will include nutrition analysis for the recipe as printed, as well as an Eat Hearty version.

The nutrition information provided in *The Best of Dierbergs* is collected from sources believed to be reliable and correct. The nutrition professionals compiling the information have made every effort to present the most accurate information available, but have undertaken no independent examination, investigation or verification of information provided by original sources. Therefore, Dierbergs assumes no liability and denies any responsibility for incorrect information resulting from the use of the nutrition information provided in *The Best of Dierbergs*.

RECIPE STANDARDS

The recipes in this cookbook were tested using the following standards unless otherwise indicated:

Eggs are large.

Butter is unsalted. Stick margarine may be substituted; do not substitute whipped butter, butter spreads or soft margarines.

Milk is 2% or higher fat; do not use fat-free or low-fat.

Dairy Products are regular or light/reduced-fat; do not use fat-free unless indicated in the recipe.

Vegetable Oil is your favorite brand.

Olive Oil is virgin for cooking, extra virgin for dressings.

Flour is all purpose.

Sugar is granulated.

Brown Sugar is firmly packed when measured.

Vanilla Extract is pure.

Salt is table salt.

Coarse Salt is kosher or sea salt.

Pepper is ground black.

Mayonnaise is regular or light/reduced-fat; do not use fat-free unless indicated in the recipe.

Preheat Oven for 10 minutes before beginning to bake.

Baking Sheets are flat without sides.

Jellyroll Pans are baking sheets with sides.

Parchment Paper makes for easy cleanup and does not need to be greased unless indicated in the recipe. It is available with aluminum foil and plastic wrap.

How Many Cooks?

How many cooks does it take to develop just one Dierbergs recipe? Well, more than you would guess! Why? Because each recipe is carefully developed, tested and scrutinized with a seven-step process by Dierbergs' (very picky) home economists and critiqued by a (very willing) taste panel. And our taste panel isn't shy in the area of feedback—we get many honest opinions with their diverse, discriminating palates. Foolproof recipes? You bet! We've done all the cooking and baking and testing and tasting. The results are wonderfully successful and wonderfully delicious.

perfect party partners

Appetizer Fare

Layered Artichoke Salsa

Spread a colorful salsa of artichokes, sun-dried tomatoes, and mild chiles over a creamy cheese layer and let the party begin. Use a vegetable peeler to create strips of parmesan for an attractive garnish.

Shaved Parmesan Cheese

Nothing beats the rich, sharp flavor of freshly grated parmesan cheese. But to give finished dishes a more distinct look, make parmesan cheese shavings. Drag a sharp vegetable peeler along the narrow edge of a wedge of cheese to make long strips. Scattered over a dip or salad, they make a sophisticated statement.

1 jar (12 ounces) marinated artichoke hearts
1/3 cup chopped sun-dried tomatoes in oil
1/3 cup diced red bell pepper
1 can (4 1/2 ounces) chopped green chiles, drained
1 can (2 1/4 ounces) sliced ripe olives, drained
1 package (8 ounces) cream cheese, softened
1/4 cup crumbled feta cheese
Shaved parmesan cheese

Drain artichokes, reserving 1/4 cup of the marinade. Coarsely chop artichokes and place in small non-metal bowl. Add sun-dried tomatoes, bell pepper, green chiles, olives, and 3 tablespoons of the reserved artichoke marinade.

In work bowl of food processor fitted with steel knife blade, combine cream cheese, feta, and remaining 1 tablespoon reserved artichoke marinade; process until smooth. Spread mixture on 10-inch serving plate. Spoon artichoke mixture over cream cheese. Garnish with shaved parmesan cheese. Serve with thinly sliced French or Italian bread.

Makes 8-12 servings

MAKE-AHEAD TIP Prepare artichoke mixture and cream cheese mixture up to 24 hours in advance. Place in separate airtight, non-metal containers; refrigerate. Assemble just before serving.

TIP If desired, light cream cheese may be used in this recipe.

Per serving

Calories 126
Fat 12 g
Cholesterol 23 mg
Sodium 249 mg
Carbohydrate 4 g
Fiber 1 g

Artichoke Squares

This is a terrific make-ahead appetizer! These flaky puff pastry squares with a cheesy artichoke topping will have everyone asking for the recipe.

technique savvy

Puff Pastry

Frozen puff pastry equals easy elegance in a box! For crisp pastry, bake it at a high temperature on a parchment-lined baking sheet. Add color and shine to the pastry by brushing it with a mixture of one egg beaten with one tablespoon water before baking. Use the egg mixture to seal edges, or to attach pastry cutouts to the top for a decorative touch.

1 jar (12 ounces) marinated artichoke hearts
8 ounces (2 cups) shredded Italian cheese blend
1 cup grated parmesan cheese
1 egg
1/2 teaspoon garlic powder
1/8 to 1/4 teaspoon hot pepper sauce
1 box (17.3 ounces) frozen puff pastry sheets, thawed

Drain artichokes, reserving 1 tablespoon of the marinade. Chop artichokes. In large bowl, combine artichokes and cheeses. In small bowl, beat together reserved marinade, egg, garlic powder, and hot sauce. On lightly floured surface, roll each sheet of pastry into 10-inch square. Brush both sheets with some of the egg mixture. Cut pastry into 2-inch squares. Place squares on parchment-lined baking sheets. Toss remaining egg mixture with artichoke mixture. Form about 1 teaspoon artichoke mixture into ball; place on pastry square. Repeat with remaining artichoke mixture and pastry squares. Bake in 400°F oven until golden brown, about 10 to 12 minutes. Serve warm.

Makes 50 appetizers

MAKE-AHEAD TIP Assemble artichoke squares; do not bake. Place on baking sheets in single layer and freeze until firm, about 1 hour. Transfer to airtight container; freeze for up to 1 month. Bake from frozen state in 400°F oven until golden brown, about 12 to 15 minutes.

Per 2 appetizers

Calories 160
Fat 11 g
Cholesterol 18 mg
Sodium 231 mg
Carbohydrate 10 g
Fiber <1 g

Cucumber Tea Sandwiches

One of our most popular recipes, this appetizer is truly a Dierbergs classic. These sandwiches are crisp, cool, and guaranteed to disappear!

1 large clove garlic

2 packages (8 ounces each) cream cheese, softened

1/4 cup snipped fresh chives

2 teaspoons grated lemon peel

1/2 teaspoon coarse salt

1/4 teaspoon ground white pepper

1 loaf (12 to 16 ounces) cocktail bread (rye, white, sourdough, or pumpernickel)

1 medium cucumber, very thinly sliced

Radishes and fresh chives for garnish (optional)

Fit food processor with steel knife blade. With machine running, drop garlic through feed tube; process until finely chopped. Add cream cheese; process until smooth. Add chives, lemon peel, salt, and pepper; process until combined. Cover and refrigerate several hours or overnight for flavors to blend. Spread about 2 teaspoons cream cheese mixture on each slice of bread. Top each with cucumber slice. If desired, grate rosy portion of radish and sprinkle over cucumber. Garnish with chives.

Makes 2 1/2 dozen appetizers

TIP If desired, light cream cheese may be used in this recipe.

Seeding a Cucumber

It is not necessary to peel cucumbers. If the skin is waxy, you can remove the peel, or rake it lengthwise with fork tines for a decorative pattern. Removing seeds from a cucumber makes them more enjoyable to eat, and will also help prevent a soggy dish. Cut cucumber in half lengthwise. Use a small spoon or melon ball cutter to scrape out the seeds.

Per 2 appetizers

Calories 165

Fat 11 g

Cholesterol 33 mg

Sodium 352 mg

Carbohydrate 13 g

Fiber 2 g

Cranberry Topped Brie

Warm cranberry chutney—kissed with Amaretto—transforms a wedge of creamy brie into an elegant appetizer.

ingredient savvy

Brie Cheese

Brie (BREE) is an elegant cheese, with an edible soft white rind and a mellow, creamy interior. Perfectly ripe brie will give to gentle pressure, and should be used within a few days of purchase. To best enjoy its mild flavor and slight earthy overtones, soften brie at room temperature and serve it with fresh fruit and nuts. Or bake it and spread the warm melted cheese on crackers or crusty bread.

1 cup fresh cranberries
1/3 cup sugar
1/4 cup water
1/2 cup chopped pear
1 tablespoon almond-flavored
    liqueur (Amaretto), or
    1/2 teaspoon almond extract
1 wedge (8 ounces) brie cheese,
    at room temperature

In medium saucepan, combine cranberries, sugar, and water. Bring to a boil over medium-high heat. Cook for 5 minutes, stirring occasionally. Stir in pear and liqueur. Cook for 2 minutes. Unwrap brie; do not remove rind. Place on serving plate. Spoon hot cranberry mixture over brie. Serve with French bread or crackers.

Makes 8 servings

MAKE-AHEAD TIP Prepare cranberry sauce and refrigerate for up to 2 days. Warm in microwave before spooning over brie.

Per serving

Calories 147
Fat 9 g
Cholesterol 20 mg
Sodium 123 mg
Carbohydrate 12 g
Fiber 1 g

Creamy Roasted Garlic Dip

Serve this rich and creamy spread as a warm welcome to your guests. Roasting the garlic mellows its flavor and brings out its natural sweetness.

ingredient savvy

Shallots

Shallots, like onion and garlic, are part of the lily family. They have a subtle flavor that doesn't overpower. The head often has two cloves, each covered with a thin, papery skin. When a recipe calls for one shallot, peel and use as many cloves as you find inside. Shallots are available year-round. Store in a cool, dry, well-ventilated place for up to a month.

14 cloves garlic (about 1 head), peeled and sliced

1 cup sliced shallot (about 3 to 4)

2 tablespoons olive oil

1 package (8 ounces) cream cheese, softened

1 package (6 ounces) goat cheese, softened

1/2 cup dairy sour cream

1 teaspoon Cajun/Creole seasoning

2 tablespoons snipped fresh chives

Place garlic and shallot on foil-lined baking sheet. Drizzle with olive oil. Bake in 400°F oven, stirring occasionally until very soft and lightly browned, about 10 to 15 minutes. Place cheeses, sour cream, and seasoning in work bowl of food processor fitted with steel knife blade; process until smooth. Add roasted garlic and shallot; pulse until just combined. Spread mixture in shallow baking dish. Bake in 400°F oven until hot and bubbly, about 15 to 20 minutes. Sprinkle chives over top. Serve warm with slices of toasted French bread or fresh vegetable dippers.

Makes 2 1/2 cups

TIP If desired, light cream cheese may be used in this recipe.

Per 2 tablespoons

Calories 94

Fat 8 g

Cholesterol 19 mg

Sodium 127 mg

Carbohydrate 3 g

Fiber <1 g

Italian Stuffed Mushrooms

Stuffed mushrooms are simple yet stylish, and right at home at any gathering. Filled with sun-dried tomatoes, nutty asiago, and fragrant rosemary, they capture the sunny flavors of the Mediterranean.

1 pound large mushrooms (20 to 24)
2 cups fine fresh bread crumbs
1/2 cup sun-dried tomatoes in oil, drained
1/2 cup grated asiago cheese (divided)
2 cloves garlic
1 teaspoon chopped fresh rosemary
1/4 teaspoon salt
1/8 teaspoon ground black pepper
Fresh rosemary sprigs for garnish

Rinse mushrooms and pat dry; remove and reserve stems. Arrange caps, stem-side up, in jellyroll pan that has been coated with no-stick cooking spray. In work bowl of food processor fitted with steel knife blade, combine mushroom stems, bread crumbs, sun-dried tomatoes, 1/4 cup of the cheese, garlic, rosemary, salt, and pepper; pulse until mixture begins to hold together. Fill caps with crumb mixture. Bake in 375°F oven until crumbs are light brown, about 15 minutes. Sprinkle with remaining 1/4 cup cheese. Bake until cheese melts, about 2 minutes. Garnish with rosemary sprigs.

Makes 20-24 appetizers

ingredient savvy

Fresh Bread Crumbs

Freeze scraps of bread and keep on hand for fresh bread crumbs any time. Trim crusts, if desired, and place the bread in a blender or food processor, a few pieces at a time, and pulse. Because they have a lighter, coarser texture than dry bread crumbs, they can't be substituted in equal amounts one for the other. Fresh bread crumbs may be frozen for up to six months.

Per 2 appetizers

Calories 57
Fat 3 g
Cholesterol 4 mg
Sodium 170 mg
Carbohydrate 6 g
Fiber 1 g

Sweet Vidalia Bruschetta

You'll love this rustic Italian appetizer of sweet caramelized onions and crusty bread. A dash of Cajun spice makes it even more inviting.

ingredient savvy

Vidalia Onions

Vidalia onions have an exceptionally sweet, mild flavor. Their high moisture content makes them perishable, so eat them soon after purchase. Vidalias are delicious fried as onion rings, raw on sandwiches, or caramelized for topping burgers. They have a short growing season, so enjoy them in early summer when they are in season. Choose Maui or red onions when Vidalias are not available.

3 tablespoons butter
3 cups chopped Vidalia onion
1 tablespoon brown sugar
1 teaspoon Cajun/Creole seasoning
1 Roma tomato, finely chopped
4 ounces (1 cup) shredded Italian
  cheese blend
Thinly sliced French baguette

In medium skillet, melt butter over medium-high heat. Stir in onion, brown sugar, and seasoning; cook, stirring frequently until golden brown and caramelized, about 15 to 20 minutes. In medium bowl, stir together caramelized onion, tomato, and cheese. Place about 1 tablespoon on each bread slice. Place on foil-lined baking sheet. Broil until cheese melts, about 1 minute.

Makes about 32 appetizers

Per 2 appetizers, bread sliced $1/4$-inch thick

Calories 72
Fat 4 g
Cholesterol 11 mg
Sodium 168 mg
Carbohydrate 7 g
Fiber 1 g

Greek Spinach Tart

Tangy feta cheese and plenty of fresh dill accent this streamlined version of the classic Greek appetizer. A rich mustard sauce is the perfect accompaniment.

1 package (15 ounces) refrigerated
    pie crusts
10 ounces baby spinach
1/2 cup dairy sour cream
2 ounces (1/2 cup) crumbled
    feta cheese
1 egg
2 teaspoons milk
2 tablespoons fresh dill weed,
    or 2 teaspoons dried
1/2 teaspoon ground black pepper
Italian seasoned bread crumbs
Creamy Mustard Sauce
    (recipe follows)

Place one of the crusts on parchment-lined baking sheet. Roll to smooth creases; set aside. Place spinach in large microwave-safe bowl; cover with plastic wrap. Microwave (high) for 2 minutes; drain and squeeze moisture from spinach. Return spinach to bowl and stir in sour cream and feta cheese; set aside. Place egg in small bowl. Remove 1 teaspoon of the yolk; place in custard cup and add milk. Stir to blend and set aside. Add remainder of the egg, dill, and pepper to spinach mixture. Brush crust with egg yolk mixture. Spread spinach mixture over crust, leaving about 3/4 inch around edge. Roll remaining crust to smooth creases; place over spinach and seal edges. If desired, flute edges or press with tines of fork. Brush top crust with remaining egg yolk mixture. Sprinkle bread crumbs over top. Bake in 425°F oven until golden brown, about 20 to 25 minutes. Cool for 5 minutes before cutting into wedges. Serve with Creamy Mustard Sauce.

Makes 12 appetizers or 6 luncheon servings

Creamy Mustard Sauce

1/2 cup dairy sour cream
2 teaspoons dijon-style mustard
1 teaspoon fresh dill weed, or
    1/4 teaspoon dried

In small bowl, combine all ingredients; stir to blend. Serve at room temperature.

Makes 1/2 cup sauce

TIP If desired, substitute Honey Mustard Sauce from Dierbergs Deli.

contributed by

Lorene Greer

Lorene Greer, Prepared Foods Manager for Dierbergs Deli, develops a wide variety of delicious fresh-prepared, take-out specialties. Lorene was formerly a School of Cooking Manager and co-host of *Dierbergs Presents Everybody Cooks®* television show, where she makes occasional guest appearances. When it comes to throwing a stylish party on a busy schedule, Lorene likes to save time by using prepared Deli items as ingredients in recipes. Her Greek Spinach Tart is among her favorite party-starters.

Per appetizer with sauce

Calories 222
Fat 14 g
Cholesterol 34 mg
Sodium 222 mg
Carbohydrate 19 g
Fiber 1 g

Triple Cheese Torta

This colorful, layered appetizer makes a beautiful centerpiece for your party table.

1 cup loosely packed baby spinach
1 package (3/4 ounce) fresh basil
1 to 2 cloves garlic, minced
2 tablespoons olive oil
1/2 cup grated parmesan or
    asiago cheese
Salt and pepper to taste
1 package (8 ounces) cream
    cheese, softened
1 package (4 ounces) goat
    cheese, softened
1/4 cup thinly sliced sun-dried
    tomatoes in oil, well drained
1/4 cup finely chopped walnuts

In work bowl of food processor fitted with steel knife blade, combine spinach, basil, and garlic; process until finely chopped. With machine running, pour olive oil through feed tube in slow steady stream. Add parmesan and process until almost smooth. Season with salt and pepper. In medium bowl, stir together cream cheese and goat cheese until well blended and smooth.

Line 3-cup bowl with plastic wrap, leaving 4-inch overhang. Spread 1/3 of the cream cheese mixture in bottom of bowl. Spread half of spinach mixture over cheese. Top with half of the sun-dried tomatoes. Sprinkle half of the walnuts over top. Drop 1/2 of the remaining cream cheese mixture by spoonfuls over tomatoes and walnuts. Carefully spread to even layer. Repeat layering with remaining spinach mixture, sun-dried tomatoes, walnuts, and cream cheese mixture. Fold plastic over top of spread. Press gently to compact. Refrigerate for 2 to 3 hours or overnight. (Spread will be firmer and easier to slice if thoroughly chilled.)

Unfold plastic and invert torta onto plate. Remove bowl and plastic wrap. Serve with toasted Italian bread, bagel chips, flat bread, or focaccia.

Makes about 2 1/2 cups

ingredient savvy

Goat Cheese

The mildly tart flavor of goat cheese is a delightful change of pace. Also known as chèvre (SHEV-ruh), it may be made entirely from goat's milk or in combination with cow's milk. Goat cheeses range from moist and creamy to dry and somewhat firm. Follow the "use by" date on the package, or keep no more than two weeks from date of purchase.

Per 2 tablespoons

Calories 90
Fat 8 g
Cholesterol 17 mg
Sodium 91 mg
Carbohydrate 1 g
Fiber <1 g

Southwest Appetizer Cheesecake

Cheesecake isn't just for dessert anymore. Spiced just right, this creamy appetizer spread is perfect for any occasion.

technique savvy

Mini Springform Pans

To make a 6-inch springform pan, tear off a 24-inch piece of heavy-duty aluminum foil; fold in half lengthwise. Now fold in thirds to make a 3×24-inch band. Cut 3/4-inch slits, 1 inch apart, along one edge. Cut a 6-inch circle out of cardboard; cover with heavy-duty foil. Place circle smooth-side down on an inverted can for support. To form sides, shape foil band around it with slits extending above the circle. Fold slits flat and tape. Remove can; fold band ends together tightly.

Per 2 tablespoons

Calories 112
Fat 10 g
Cholesterol 43 mg
Sodium 167 mg
Carbohydrate 3 g
Fiber <1 g

1 cup finely crushed tortilla chips
3 tablespoons butter or margarine, melted
3 packages (8 ounces each) cream cheese, softened
4 eggs, at room temperature
8 ounces (2 cups) shredded sharp cheddar cheese
1 can (9 ounces) jalapeño-cheddar cheese dip
1 can (4 1/2 ounces) chopped green chiles or jalapeños, drained
1 cup dairy sour cream
1 cup seeded and chopped tomato
1/2 cup thinly sliced green onion
1 can (4 ounces) sliced ripe olives, drained

In medium bowl, combine crushed chips and butter. Press half of the mixture into each of two 6-inch springform pans (see sidebar). Place pans on baking sheet. Bake in 325°F oven for 10 minutes. In work bowl of food processor fitted with steel knife blade or in large mixer bowl, process cream cheese until smooth. Add eggs, one at a time, processing well after each addition. Add shredded cheddar and dip; process until blended. Fold in green chiles. Pour half of the mixture over each prepared crust. Bake in 325°F oven until almost set, about 40 to 45 minutes. Cool completely in springform pans on wire rack. Cover and refrigerate overnight.

Before serving, remove cakes from pans; place on serving plates. Spread 1/2 cup sour cream over each cheesecake. In small bowl, combine tomato, green onion, and olives; sprinkle half of the mixture evenly over each cheesecake. Serve with tortilla chips.

Makes two 6-inch cheesecakes

TIP Cheesecake may be baked in one 9-inch springform pan. Increase baking time to 55 to 60 minutes or until almost set.

Sweet and Sassy Wings

These wings are everything you're looking for—sweet, sticky, and oh, so good!

5 pounds frozen chicken wing
    portions or drummettes
1 cup cola-type soda (not diet)
1 cup Kansas City-style barbecue
    sauce
1/4 cup firmly packed brown sugar
2 to 3 tablespoons hot pepper sauce
4 cloves garlic, minced

Place half of frozen wings in single layer on rack of broiler pan that has been coated with no-stick cooking spray. Bake in 400°F oven for 25 minutes. Turn wings and bake until lightly browned and thoroughly cooked, about 20 minutes; set aside. Repeat with remaining wings. In small saucepan, combine remaining ingredients. Bring to a boil over medium-high heat. Reduce heat and simmer, stirring frequently, until sauce reduces and thickens, about 15 minutes. Place cooked wings in large roasting pan or Dutch oven. Pour sauce over. Cover and cook in 350°F oven for 20 minutes, stirring occasionally.

Makes 5 pounds

MAKE-AHEAD TIP Bake wings as directed. Place in covered container and refrigerate for up to 24 hours. Place in large roasting pan. Pour sauce over. Cover and cook in 350°F oven, stirring occasionally, until heated through, about 30 minutes.

Southern-Style BBQ Sauce

Add a little Southern hospitality to your next cookout by simmering your favorite barbecue sauce with a can of cola or root beer. Soda adds sweetness and a caramel color to the sauce. Be sure to use regular soda, not diet, since the artificial sweeteners lose their effect when heated.

Per 2 wings

Calories 219
Fat 14 g
Cholesterol 75 mg
Sodium 425 mg
Carbohydrate 7 g
Fiber 0 g

Crab Cakes with Aïoli

Served with a rich roasted pepper or tangy lemon aïoli, crisp, golden-brown crab cakes are a special treat. Make them early in the day, refrigerate, and pop under the broiler when guests arrive.

What Is Aïoli?

Whether you say, "ay-oh-lee" or "i-oh-lee," this very garlicky mayonnaise from the Provence region in southern France is wonderful with many dishes. Aïoli is the perfect partner to fish, meats, and vegetables. Garlic is a must for this recipe, and you can use a variety of ingredients for additional flavor.

Per 2 appetizers

Calories 103
Fat 7 g
Cholesterol 47 mg
Sodium 356 mg
Carbohydrate 8 g
Fiber 1 g

Per 2 tablespoons

Calories 139
Fat 15 g
Cholesterol 7 mg
Sodium 112 mg
Carbohydrate 2 g
Fiber <1 g

1 egg, slightly beaten
1/4 cup mayonnaise
1/4 cup finely chopped celery
1/4 cup finely chopped onion
1 tablespoon minced fresh
    Italian parsley
1 tablespoon fresh lemon juice
2 teaspoons Old Bay seafood
    seasoning
2 cans (6.5 ounces each) crabmeat,
    drained and flaked
2 cups panko (Japanese bread
    crumbs) (divided)
Roasted Red Pepper Aïoli (recipe
    follows) or Lemon Aïoli
    (page 107)

In large bowl, combine all ingredients except crabmeat, bread crumbs, and aïoli; stir until well blended. Add crabmeat and 3/4 cup of the bread crumbs. Stir until evenly moistened; let stand 10 minutes. Shape crab mixture into cakes, using 1 tablespoon for each cake; coat with remaining bread crumbs. Place crab cakes on foil-lined baking sheet that has been coated with no-stick cooking spray. Lightly coat tops of crab cakes with cooking spray. Broil until crumbs are golden brown, about 2 to 3 minutes per side. Let stand 1 to 2 minutes. Serve warm with aïoli.

Makes about 2 dozen appetizers

Roasted Red Pepper Aïoli

3 cloves garlic
1 cup mayonnaise
1 red bell pepper, roasted, with
    seeds and skin removed
2 tablespoons minced fresh Italian
    parsley
1 tablespoon dijon-style mustard
1 teaspoon sugar
1 teaspoon fresh lemon juice

Fit food processor with steel knife blade. With machine running, drop garlic through feed tube and process until finely chopped. Add remaining ingredients; pulse until well mixed. Place in covered container and refrigerate for up to 3 days.

Makes about 1 1/2 cups

Rosemary Shrimp Spiedini

Elegant simplicity defines this delectable combination of shrimp, rosemary, lemon, and garlic. For a dramatic presentation, skewer the shrimp on sprigs of fresh rosemary.

technique savvy

Skewers

Bamboo skewers need to soak in water for about ten minutes to prevent charring during cooking. Food tends to twirl on metal skewers. Choose flat metal to minimize twirling. If they are round, try inserting two skewers parallel to one another. Place foods with similar textures on the same skewer. Cut food into uniform sizes and leave a little space between pieces for even cooking.

12 sprigs fresh rosemary
1 pound large shrimp
3 tablespoons olive oil
2 tablespoons butter, melted
1 to 2 cloves garlic, minced
1/2 cup Italian seasoned
   bread crumbs
1/4 cup grated parmesan cheese
2 teaspoons grated lemon peel

Hold each rosemary sprig between thumb and forefinger about 1 inch from tip of sprig. Slide fingers down stem to strip leaves and make skewers. Soak rosemary stem skewers in cold water for at least 10 minutes to prevent charring during cooking. Peel and devein shrimp, leaving tails intact. Thread 2 or 3 shrimp onto each rosemary skewer. In shallow pie plate, combine olive oil, butter, and garlic. In another shallow pie plate, stir together bread crumbs, parmesan, and lemon peel. Roll each skewer of shrimp in oil mixture. Roll in crumb mixture, coating both sides. Place skewers on oiled grid over medium-high heat; grill until shrimp are opaque and coating is lightly browned, about 2 to 3 minutes per side.

Makes 1 dozen appetizers

TIP If desired, shrimp may be grilled on metal or bamboo skewers. Add 1 teaspoon finely chopped fresh rosemary to crumb mixture.

Per 2 appetizers

Calories 228
Fat 13 g
Cholesterol 129 mg
Sodium 457 mg
Carbohydrate 8 g
Fiber 1 g

Sesame Meatballs with Sweet and Sour Sauce

No appetizer buffet is complete without meatballs! Fresh ginger and red pepper flakes give these plenty of zip.

technique savvy

Handling Ground Beef

When mixing ground beef for shaping into meatballs or patties, handle with care. Stir just enough to incorporate other ingredients, and shape gently. Overhandling causes beef to shrink and toughen during cooking. Store ground beef in the coldest part of the refrigerator for up to two days, or freeze for up to six months.

Per 2 meatballs with sauce

Calories 95
Fat 3 g
Cholesterol 30 mg
Sodium 263 mg
Carbohydrate 9 g
Fiber <1 g

1/3 cup milk
1/4 cup Italian seasoned bread
    crumbs
1 pound lean ground beef
1 egg, slightly beaten
1/2 cup thinly sliced green onion
2 large cloves garlic, minced
2 tablespoons sesame seed, toasted
1 tablespoon minced fresh
    ginger root
1/2 teaspoon salt
1/4 teaspoon ground black pepper
Sweet and Sour Sauce
    (recipe follows)

In large bowl, combine milk and bread crumbs; let stand until crumbs soften, about 2 minutes. Stir in remaining ingredients except Sweet and Sour Sauce. Shape into 1-inch balls. Place on foil-lined jellyroll pan. Bake in 350°F oven until browned and cooked through, about 15 to 20 minutes. Place meatballs in serving dish. Pour Sweet and Sour Sauce over meatballs.

Makes 32 meatballs

Sweet and Sour Sauce

1/2 cup firmly packed brown sugar
2 tablespoons cornstarch
1 tablespoon minced fresh
    ginger root
1/4 teaspoon crushed red
    pepper flakes
1/2 cup beef broth
1/2 cup rice vinegar or white
    wine vinegar
2 tablespoons soy sauce
2 tablespoons dry sherry

In small saucepan, combine brown sugar, cornstarch, ginger, and pepper flakes. Stir in remaining ingredients. Cook over medium-high heat, stirring occasionally, until sauce comes to a boil and thickens.

Makes 1 1/2 cups

Peppered Pork Sandwiches

A dollop of the zesty horseradish sauce gives these miniature sandwiches a little extra flair. Place all the makings on the table and let guests assemble their own sandwiches.

1 pork tenderloin
   (about 1¼ pounds)
2 tablespoons dijon-style mustard
1 tablespoon cracked black pepper
1 loaf (8 ounces) French baguette,
   thinly sliced
Granny Smith Horseradish Sauce
   (recipe follows)

Trim fat and silver skin from tenderloin. Spread mustard over surface of pork. Place pepper on sheet of waxed paper. Roll pork in pepper to coat. Place pork on rack in foil-lined shallow roasting pan. Roast in 350°F oven until internal temperature is 155°F, about 40 to 45 minutes. (Meat will be slightly pink.) Let stand 10 minutes before slicing very thinly. Arrange on serving platter, and surround with sliced French bread. Serve with Granny Smith Horseradish Sauce.

Makes 18-20 appetizers

MAKE-AHEAD TIP Cook pork, slice, and arrange on serving platter up to 24 hours in advance. Cover and chill. Remove from refrigerator 30 minutes before serving.

Silver Skin

Silver skin is a thin, translucent membrane that covers pork tenderloin. It is best to remove and discard it before cooking to make the meat more tender and prevent it from curling. Use a sharp knife to loosen the silver skin and gently scrape it away; or grasp it with a paper towel and pull it from the tenderloin.

Granny Smith Horseradish Sauce

1 cup mayonnaise
1 Granny Smith apple, peeled,
   cored, and coarsely grated
2 tablespoons prepared horseradish
¼ teaspoon dried dill weed

In medium bowl, combine all ingredients. Stir to blend. Cover and chill several hours or up to 3 days.

Makes about 1½ cups

Per appetizer with sauce

Calories 113
Fat 8 g
Cholesterol 19 mg
Sodium 92 mg
Carbohydrate 3 g
Fiber <1 g

Thai Spring Rolls

Crisp fillo rolls bursting with lively Asian flavors will surprise and delight your guests.

Fillo Dough

No matter what you wrap in it, layers of crisp, flaky fillo make anything more inviting. Defrost fillo completely by placing the sealed package in the refrigerator overnight. Rapid thawing at room temperature may cause dough to dry and crack. As you work, cover extra sheets of fillo with plastic wrap and a slightly damp cloth towel to prevent drying. Unused fillo may be tightly wrapped and refrozen once.

8 ounces reduced-fat pork sausage, cooked and drained
1/2 cup finely chopped celery
1/3 cup finely chopped onion
1/3 cup shredded carrots
1/3 cup finely chopped mushrooms
2 cloves garlic, minced
2 tablespoons teriyaki sauce
1/2 teaspoon ground ginger
8 ounces (1/2 of 16-ounce twin package) frozen fillo dough, thawed in refrigerator overnight
1/4 cup butter, melted, or no-stick cooking spray
Thai Dipping Sauce (recipe follows)

In large bowl, combine cooked sausage, celery, onion, carrots, mushrooms, garlic, teriyaki sauce, and ginger; set aside.

Unroll fillo onto work surface. Cover completely with plastic wrap. Place 1 sheet fillo on clean dry surface; brush with butter or coat with cooking spray. Top with 3 more fillo sheets, brushing each sheet with butter. Cut fillo stack in half crosswise to make two 7×9-inch rectangles. Place 1/4 cup filling on lower third of each rectangle. Fold in sides of fillo to enclose filling. Starting at filling end, roll up jellyroll style. Place seam-side down on parchment-lined baking sheet. Brush with butter or coat with cooking spray. Repeat procedure 4 times with remaining fillo and filling. Bake in 375°F oven until fillo is golden brown, about 20 to 22 minutes. Serve with Thai Dipping Sauce.

Makes 10 appetizers

Per appetizer

Calories 207
Fat 11 g
Cholesterol 29 mg
Sodium 798 mg
Carbohydrate 21 g
Fiber 1 g

Thai Dipping Sauce

1/2 cup chicken broth
1/2 cup white wine vinegar
1/3 cup teriyaki sauce
1/4 cup firmly packed brown sugar
3 cloves garlic, minced
1 tablespoon cornstarch
1 to 2 teaspoons hot pepper sauce

In medium saucepan, whisk together all sauce ingredients over medium-high heat; cook until thickened, about 3 to 4 minutes.

Makes 1 1/2 cups

MAKE-AHEAD TIP Assemble rolls; do not bake. Place on baking sheet; cover and freeze until firm, about 1 hour. Transfer to airtight container and freeze for up to 1 month. Bake from frozen state in 375°F oven until fillo is golden brown, about 25 to 27 minutes.

hearty and heartwarming

Soups, Sandwiches, and Breads

Chicken and Wild Rice Soup

Filled with chunks of tender chicken and savory wild rice, this creamy soup is rich and satisfying. Add a simple green salad for a complete meal.

3 cans (14 ounces each) reduced-sodium chicken broth (divided)
1 package (6 ounces) long grain and wild rice (original recipe)
1 pound boneless, skinless chicken breast halves, cut into 1/2-inch pieces
1 package (10 ounces) frozen chopped broccoli
3 tablespoons flour
2 cups half-and-half

Set 1/2 cup of the broth aside. In large saucepan, stir together remaining broth and rice with its seasonings; cover and bring to a boil. Reduce heat; simmer for 10 minutes, stirring occasionally. Stir in chicken and broccoli. Cover and simmer, stirring occasionally until chicken is cooked and rice is tender, about 15 minutes. Stir flour into reserved broth. Add to soup; bring to a boil and cook, stirring constantly until slightly thickened. Reduce heat and stir in half-and-half; cook until heated through, about 3 to 4 minutes.

Makes 4-6 servings

Spicy White Chili

A favorite on many restaurant menus, this zesty style of chili is full of tender chunks of chicken. Take it along to your next tailgate party, too!

1 pound boneless, skinless chicken
    breast halves
1 tablespoon olive oil
3/4 cup chopped onion
2 cloves garlic, minced
2 cans (14 ounces each) chicken
    broth (divided)
2 teaspoons cornstarch
3 cans (15 ounces each) cannellini
    beans, rinsed and drained
2 cans (4 1/2 ounces each) chopped
    green chiles
1 1/2 teaspoons ground cumin
1 to 1 1/2 teaspoons ground
    red pepper
1 teaspoon dried oregano
Toppings—shredded cheddar, dairy
    sour cream, chopped tomatoes,
    sliced green onions
Tortilla chips (optional)

Cut chicken into bite-sized pieces. In heavy 4-quart saucepan, heat olive oil over medium-high heat. Add chicken; cook for 2 minutes. Add onion and garlic; cook for 2 minutes. In small bowl, combine 1/4 cup of the broth with the cornstarch. Add to chicken mixture along with remaining broth, beans, chiles, and seasonings. Cover and bring to a boil. Uncover, reduce heat, and simmer for 15 minutes. Top each serving as desired and serve with tortilla chips.

Makes 8-10 servings

ingredient savvy

Fresh Chiles

From mild to wild, fresh chiles are readily available year-round. Generally, the smaller the chile and the more pointed the tip, the hotter the variety. Fresh poblanos, also known as green chiles, are very mild. Jalapeños range from hot to very hot. And habañeros are among the hottest of all. The oils in peppers can sting eyes and skin. Wear disposable gloves when seeding fresh chiles and immediately wash your hands to prevent irritation.

**Per serving
without toppings**

Calories 181
Fat 3 g
Cholesterol 27 mg
Sodium 627 mg
Carbohydrate 21 g
Fiber 6 g

Szechuan Chicken Soup

A classic comfort food gets a little kick from Szechuan seasoning. Chinese noodles give it a real homemade touch.

4 cans (14 ounces each) reduced-sodium chicken broth

2 carrots, cut into matchstick-sized pieces

1 cup chopped celery

4 teaspoons Szechuan seasoning

8 ounces fresh Chinese noodles or egg noodles

4 teaspoons cornstarch

2 tablespoons water

1/2 pound boneless, skinless chicken breast halves, cooked and diced

2 green onions including green tops, thinly sliced on the diagonal

In large saucepan, combine broth, carrots, celery, and seasoning; bring to a boil over medium-high heat. Reduce heat, cover, and simmer for 5 minutes. Add noodles and simmer until noodles are tender, about 10 minutes. In small bowl, stir cornstarch and water until smooth. Gradually stir into soup. Add chicken and green onions; cook until slightly thickened, about 2 to 3 minutes.

Makes 8 servings

TIP Look for fresh Chinese noodles in the produce department.

technique savvy

How to Microwave Chicken

When a recipe calls for cooked chicken, cook it in the microwave! Place boneless, skinless chicken breasts in a microwave-safe dish. Cover with plastic wrap and vent to let steam escape. Microwave on high for six minutes per pound, rearranging pieces halfway through cooking time, and let stand for five minutes. The internal temperature should be 165°F. Add another minute or two of cooking if needed.

Per serving

Calories 166

Fat 1 g

Cholesterol 34 mg

Sodium 570 mg

Carbohydrate 20 g

Fiber 1 g

Tortilla Soup

The whole family will love this colorful fiesta-in-a-bowl! Set out all the toppings and let everyone choose their favorites. It's a great way to use turkey leftovers!

ingredient savvy

Lower-Sodium Beans

Drain and rinse canned beans before adding them to soup, chili, or other recipes. You'll keep all the convenience and health benefits while eliminating about one-third of the sodium. For the best texture, add canned beans toward the end of cooking time.

1 small onion, chopped
2 cloves garlic, minced
1 tablespoon vegetable oil
3 to 4 cups diced cooked turkey
    or chicken
1 box (32 ounces) chicken broth
2 cups frozen corn
1 can (15 ounces) black beans,
    rinsed and drained
1 can (14 1/2 ounces) diced tomatoes
    and green chiles
1 teaspoon ground cumin
Tortilla chips, coarsely crushed
Toppings—shredded Mexican
    cheese blend, diced avocado,
    sour cream, lime wedges,
    chopped fresh cilantro,
    shredded lettuce

In large saucepan, cook onion and garlic in oil over medium-high heat until tender, about 3 minutes. Add remaining ingredients except tortilla chips and toppings; bring to a boil. Reduce heat and simmer for 10 to 15 minutes. Sprinkle tortilla chips over each serving and top as desired.

Makes 6-8 servings

Per serving without tortilla chips or toppings

Calories 245
Fat 8 g
Cholesterol 49 mg
Sodium 991 mg
Carbohydrate 23 g
Fiber 5 g

Cheesy Cheddar Chowder

Nothing warms up a blustery day like a bowl of this hearty soup. The mellow flavor of cheddar cheese makes this one a family favorite.

1 medium potato, peeled and diced

2 ribs celery, thinly sliced

2 carrots, chopped

1 small onion, chopped

3 tablespoons butter or margarine

1 can (14 ounces) chicken broth

3 tablespoons flour

2 cups milk (divided)

1 cup diced ham (optional)

8 ounces (2 cups) finely shredded cheddar cheese

In large heavy saucepan, cook potato, celery, carrots, and onion in butter over medium-high heat for 5 minutes or until onion is translucent. Add broth; bring to a boil. Reduce heat, cover, and simmer until vegetables are tender, about 12 minutes. In small bowl, stir flour into $1/4$ cup of the milk to make thin paste. Gradually stir into vegetables. Stir in remaining milk. Increase heat to medium-high; cook, stirring frequently until chowder begins to thicken. If desired, stir in ham. Remove from heat; stir in cheese until melted.

Makes 4-6 servings

TIP It is important to add cheese after removing soup from heat to prevent curdling.

ingredient savvy

Reduced-Sodium Broth

Since canned foods contain significant amounts of salt, consider substituting reduced-sodium broth in any recipe calling for canned broth. Taste your recipe as it cooks and adjust the seasonings near the end of the cooking time.

Per serving

Calories 292

Fat 21 g

Cholesterol 63 mg

Sodium 627 mg

Carbohydrate 14 g

Fiber 1 g

Shrimp Poblano Chowder

Mild poblano chiles add gentle heat to this hearty, colorful chowder. Roasting the chile gives it a slightly smoky flavor.

ingredient savvy

Shrimp

Shrimp is sold by size or "count:" jumbo (16-20 per pound), extra-large (26-30), and large (43-50). Larger shrimp are more expensive, but make a more impressive presentation and are less work to clean. Cooking shrimp in the shell gives the best flavor and texture. To devein shrimp in the shell, use kitchen shears to cut along the back edge of the shell. Remove the vein under cold running water.

1 bag (12 ounces) frozen cooked, peeled, and deveined medium shrimp
1 large poblano pepper, halved and seeded
1 tablespoon olive oil
1/2 cup chopped onion
1 clove garlic, minced
1 tablespoon chili powder
1 teaspoon ground cumin
2 tablespoons flour
2 cans (14 ounces each) chicken broth
1 can (15 ounces) crushed tomatoes
1/2 cup medium barley
1 cup frozen corn, thawed
4 ounces (1 cup) shredded sharp cheddar cheese
Crispy Tortilla Strips (recipe follows)

Thaw shrimp according to package directions. Cut each shrimp in half, if desired; set aside. Place poblano pepper, skin-side up, on foil-lined baking sheet; broil until skin is black and blistered. Place pepper in small reclosable plastic bag; seal and let steam for 10 minutes or until skin has softened. Remove and discard blackened skin. Chop pepper; set aside.

In large saucepan, heat olive oil over medium-high heat. Add onion, garlic, chili powder, and cumin. Cook stirring frequently until onion softens, about 2 minutes. Stir in flour and cook for 1 minute. Stir in chicken broth, tomatoes, and barley; bring to a boil. Reduce heat, cover, and simmer, stirring occasionally until barley is tender, about 35 to 40 minutes. Stir in shrimp, corn, and roasted pepper; cook until heated through. Remove from heat. Stir in cheese until melted. Top each serving with Crispy Tortilla Strips.

Makes 6-8 servings

Crispy Tortilla Strips

Using scissors, cut 3 corn tortillas into 3×1/4-inch strips. In small bowl, combine 1 teaspoon chili powder and 1/4 teaspoon cumin. In deep skillet, heat 1/2 inch of oil over medium-high heat. Cook tortilla strips in small batches until crisp, about 1 to 2 minutes. Immediately remove from oil with slotted spoon. Drain on paper towels; sprinkle spice mixture over hot strips. Cool completely. Store in airtight container for up to 3 days.

Per serving with 3 tablespoons tortilla strips

Calories 267
Fat 11 g
Cholesterol 97 mg
Sodium 795 mg
Carbohydrate 28 g
Fiber 5 g

Fresh Asparagus Soup

Great as a first course or light lunch, this velvety soup is the perfect way to savor fresh, tender asparagus.

ingredient savvy

Fresh Asparagus

Asparagus is a welcome harbinger of spring. Choose firm, bright green stalks with tightly closed purple-tinted buds. Asparagus can be stored for one to two days in the refrigerator. Stand the bunch upright in a container with about one inch of water, cover the tops with a plastic bag, and refrigerate. Gently snap each stalk at the bottom. It will break at the very spot where woodiness begins. Rinse with water, then steam, microwave, or grill just until crisp-tender.

1 pound fresh asparagus (divided)
1/4 cup thinly sliced green onion
1 tablespoon butter or margarine
1 1/2 tablespoons flour
1 can (14 ounces) chicken broth
1/2 cup half-and-half
1/2 teaspoon sugar
1/2 teaspoon salt
Dash ground white pepper
Grated parmesan cheese

Snap off and discard tough white ends from asparagus. Cut tips from spears, reserving stalks. In small saucepan, simmer tips in 1/2 cup water until tender, about 3 minutes. Use slotted spoon to remove tips, leaving cooking liquid in pan; set tips aside for garnish. Cut reserved stalks into 1-inch pieces. Add pieces along with green onion to saucepan and simmer until tender, about 6 minutes. Do not drain. In work bowl of food processor fitted with steel knife blade or in blender container, process asparagus mixture and cooking liquid until puréed. In medium saucepan, melt butter over medium-high heat. Stir in flour until smooth. Add broth and asparagus purée; bring to a boil. Reduce heat and simmer, stirring frequently until thickened, about 2 minutes. Stir in half-and-half, sugar, salt, and white pepper; cook until heated through. Garnish each serving with reserved asparagus tips and parmesan.

Makes 4 servings

Per serving with margarine, fat-free low-sodium broth, and fat-free half-and-half; without parmesan

Calories 75
Fat 3 g
Cholesterol 0 mg
Sodium 588 mg
Carbohydrate 8 g
Fiber 2 g

Per serving without parmesan

Calories 96
Fat 7 g
Cholesterol 20 mg
Sodium 733 mg
Carbohydrate 6 g
Fiber 2 g

Sherried Wild Mushroom Soup

A variety of mushrooms and a splash of sherry give this elegant soup a deep, rich flavor. It's the perfect start to a special dinner.

3 tablespoons butter

1 pound mushrooms (crimini, oyster, shiitake, button, or any combination), sliced

1/2 cup finely chopped shallot

3 tablespoons flour

1 can (10 1/2 ounces) condensed chicken broth

1/4 cup dry sherry

2 cups half-and-half

Dash ground nutmeg

Salt and pepper to taste

Chopped fresh Italian parsley

In large skillet, melt butter over medium-high heat. Add mushrooms and shallot; cook for 4 to 5 minutes, stirring constantly. Sprinkle flour over mushrooms; stir until evenly mixed. Gradually stir in broth and sherry; cook, stirring constantly until thickened, about 5 minutes. Gradually stir in half-and-half; cook until heated through (do not boil). Stir in nutmeg. Season with salt and pepper. Garnish each serving with chopped parsley.

Makes 6 servings

ingredient savvy

Wild Mushrooms

Wild mushrooms add interesting flavor and texture to recipes. Remove the stems from shiitake and portabella mushrooms and discard them, or save to flavor soup stock. Mushrooms absorb water like a sponge and quickly become mushy. To clean them, simply wipe them with a damp paper towel. Store mushrooms in the refrigerator in a paper bag or loosely covered to extend their life.

Per serving

Calories 229

Fat 18 g

Cholesterol 46 mg

Sodium 402 mg

Carbohydrate 12 g

Fiber 1 g

Tuscan Vegetable Soup

This warm and wonderful soup is a meal that the whole family will love. Keep the ingredients on hand for a dinner that's ready in minutes.

1 pound lean ground beef

1 small onion, chopped

1/2 cup thinly sliced celery

1 clove garlic, minced

1 can (15 1/2 ounces) diced tomatoes
   in juice

1 can (14 ounces) beef broth

1 cup thinly sliced carrots

1 teaspoon Italian herb seasoning

1 can (15 ounces) cannellini or navy
   beans, rinsed and drained

Shredded asiago cheese

In Dutch oven or large saucepan, cook ground beef, onion, celery, and garlic over medium-high heat until beef is no longer pink; drain any fat. Add tomatoes with their juice, broth, carrots, and seasoning. Bring to a boil. Reduce heat and simmer for 10 minutes or until vegetables are tender. Stir in beans. Cook until heated through, about 2 minutes. Top each serving with asiago cheese.

Makes 6 servings

c u i s i n e   s a v v y

What Is Tuscan?

Recipes from this central part of Italy are simple, rustic, and fresh, yet full of flavor. Tuscany is the home of biscotti, bruschetta, and balsamic vinegar. It is also famous for its soups, particularly those made with cannellini—tender white kidney beans.

Per serving without asiago cheese

Calories 219

Fat 6 g

Cholesterol 45 mg

Sodium 550 mg

Carbohydrate 19 g

Fiber 6 g

Double Baked Potato Soup

Like a baked potato with all of your favorite toppings, this hearty soup is a meal in itself. The combination of russet and sweet potatoes makes it deliciously different.

1 large russet potato
1 large sweet potato
2 tablespoons butter
1/4 cup flour
2 cups half-and-half
1 can (14 ounces) chicken broth
1/2 cup dairy sour cream
1/4 cup sliced green onion
Salt and ground white pepper
   to taste
6 slices bacon, diced and
   cooked crisp
2 ounces (1/2 cup) finely shredded
   sharp cheddar cheese

Scrub potatoes and pierce with fork. Bake in 400°F oven for 1 hour, or microwave (high) for 5 to 8 minutes, until cooked through. Let stand until cool enough to handle. Peel potatoes; coarsely mash and set aside. In heavy 3-quart saucepan, melt butter over medium-high heat. Whisk in flour to make thick paste. Slowly whisk in half-and-half and broth. Cook over medium heat, stirring constantly until thickened and bubbly, about 2 minutes. Add mashed potatoes, sour cream, and green onion; cook until heated through. Season with salt and pepper. Top each serving with bacon and cheese.

Makes 4-6 servings

Microwaving Bacon Bits

For crunchy bacon bits in minutes, place bacon strips in a shallow microwave-safe dish lined with paper towels. Microwave on high for I minute per slice; cool and crumble. If you're cooking a whole pound of bacon, use scissors to snip the raw bacon into 1/4-inch pieces. Place the bacon pieces in a microwave-safe bowl, cover with paper towels, and microwave on high for 12 to 15 minutes, stirring every 3 minutes, until crisp.

Per serving

Calories 317
Fat 23 g
Cholesterol 64 mg
Sodium 551 mg
Carbohydrate 20 g
Fiber 2 g

Pulled Beef Sandwiches

Beer, savory seasonings, and slow simmering make beef moist, tender, and delicious. Serve it piled high on sandwich buns, or as a change-of-pace filling for tacos.

1 boneless beef arm or chuck roast
  (3 to 4 pounds)
1 tablespoon vegetable oil
1 can (12 ounces) beer
5 large cloves garlic, minced
1 tablespoon Italian herb seasoning
1 teaspoon salt
1/2 teaspoon ground black pepper
1 cup prepared barbecue sauce
12 Kaiser rolls or buns, or
  24 dollar rolls

Trim any visible fat from meat. In Dutch oven over medium-high heat, heat oil. Add meat; cook until browned on both sides. Add beer, garlic, and seasonings; bring to a boil. Reduce heat; cover and simmer until meat pulls apart easily with fork, about 2 to 2 1/2 hours. Remove meat from pan; shred with 2 forks. Cover and refrigerate meat and liquid in separate containers for up to 3 days.

To serve, skim fat from liquid. In large saucepan, combine liquid and barbecue sauce. Add shredded beef; cover and cook over low heat, stirring occasionally, until meat is warmed through. Serve on rolls.

Makes 12 sandwiches (or 24 dollar roll sandwiches)

TIP Substitute taco sauce for barbecue sauce to make a savory taco filling.

Braising

Braising is the best way to make less-tender cuts of meat moist and tender. Trim away excess fat, brown the meat well on all sides, and add a small amount of liquid to the pan. Include something acidic, like beer, wine, soy sauce, or tomatoes to help tenderize the meat and add extra flavor. Cover and cook over low heat until the meat is tender and delicious.

Per Kaiser roll sandwich

Calories 398
Fat 17 g
Cholesterol 57 mg
Sodium 732 mg
Carbohydrate 34 g
Fiber 2 g

Mediterranean Chicken Sandwich

Crisp lettuce, colorful peppers, and thick crusty bread make these sandwiches a special treat for lunch or dinner. A creamy feta spread gives them rich Mediterranean flavor.

6 boneless, skinless chicken breast
    halves, pounded to even
    thickness
Olive oil
1 teaspoon dried oregano
1 teaspoon coarse salt
1/4 teaspoon ground black pepper
1 red bell pepper, cut into strips
1 yellow bell pepper, cut into strips
Feta Spread (recipe follows)
12 slices rosemary-olive oil bread or
    sourdough bread, lightly toasted
Romaine lettuce leaves

Place chicken on rack of broiler pan. Brush with olive oil. In small bowl, combine oregano, salt, and pepper; sprinkle half of the mixture over chicken. Broil 4 inches from heat source until lightly browned, about 4 to 5 minutes. Turn chicken over; brush with oil and sprinkle with remaining herbs. Place pepper strips on rack alongside chicken; brush with oil. Broil until internal temperature of chicken is 165°F and peppers are tender, about 4 to 5 minutes. Spread one side of each slice of bread with Feta Spread. Top with chicken, peppers, and lettuce.

Makes 6 servings

TIP If desired, serve sandwiches on Rosemary Focaccia, split in half.

ingredient savvy

Feta Cheese

Feta cheese is as common to Greek cuisine as cheddar is to American. Feta is a crumbly, white cheese with a salty, tangy flavor. It can be used in baked dishes, sprinkled over pasta, or as a topping on salads. Purchase feta in a block or crumbled. It is also available flavored with herbs.

Feta Spread

2 ounces (1/2 cup) crumbled
    feta cheese
1/2 cup mayonnaise
1 large garlic clove, minced
1 teaspoon fresh lemon juice
1/2 teaspoon dried oregano

Combine all ingredients in small bowl; stir to blend.

Makes 1 cup

**Per serving with
2 tablespoons spread**

Calories 503
Fat 22 g
Cholesterol 80 mg
Sodium 779 mg
Carbohydrate 41 g
Fiber 2 g

Recipe for Rosemary Focaccia
(pictured) on page 56

53

Portabella Pockets

The rich, meaty texture of portabella mushrooms makes them great for grilling. Add them to pita bread stuffed with savory vegetables and creamy herb cheese for a hearty, meatless sandwich.

4 portabella mushrooms (each about 4 inches in diameter), stemmed
4 thick slices sweet onion (Vidalia, Maui, red)
1 red bell pepper, halved and seeded
1/2 cup Italian or vinaigrette dressing
1 package (6 to 8 ounces) herb cream cheese spread
4 pita pockets, cut in half
Baby spinach

Place portabella mushroom caps, onion, and bell pepper in large reclosable plastic bag; add dressing. Seal bag; turn to coat. Marinate in refrigerator for up to 2 hours. Remove vegetables from marinade, reserving marinade. Place vegetables on grid over high heat. Grill, basting occasionally with marinade, until vegetables are tender, about 4 to 5 minutes per side. Cut portabellas in half and peppers into strips. Spread about 1 tablespoon of the herb cream cheese inside each pita pocket and line with spinach. Fill pockets with grilled vegetables.

Makes 4 servings

TO BROIL Place vegetables on rack of broiler pan that has been coated with no-stick cooking spray. Broil, basting occasionally with reserved marinade, until vegetables are tender, about 5 to 6 minutes per side.

Per serving

Calories 467
Fat 19 g
Cholesterol 40 mg
Sodium 1321 mg
Carbohydrate 64 g
Fiber 1 g

Garlic Grilled Cheese

Grilled cheese for grown ups! Crisp pepper bacon, diced tomatoes, and plenty of garlic transform a childhood favorite into a gourmet treat!

8 ounces havarti cheese, shredded
    (about 2 cups)
8 slices pepper-crusted bacon, diced
    and cooked crisp
1/4 cup mayonnaise
1/4 cup diced grape tomatoes
3 tablespoons thinly sliced
    green onion
3 cloves garlic, minced (divided)
8 slices pumpernickel bread
1/4 cup butter, softened

In medium bowl, combine cheese, bacon, mayonnaise, tomatoes, green onion, and 2 cloves of the minced garlic. Spread mixture evenly on 4 slices of bread. Top with remaining bread to make 4 sandwiches. In small bowl, combine butter and remaining minced garlic. Spread on both sides of sandwiches. On griddle or large skillet, cook sandwiches until nicely browned and cheese is melted, about 2 to 3 minutes per side.

Makes 4 servings

contributed by

Nancy Lorenz

Staff Home Economist Nancy Lorenz has been the School of Cooking Manager at Clarkson since 1979. Nancy credits her mom—"a fabulous cook"—as her mentor in the kitchen. The different cultures in her hometown of Winnipeg, Manitoba, serve as inspiration for her many classes and vast collection of recipes. Everyone agrees that garlic is Nancy's favorite ingredient! Customers and co-workers alike look forward to her annual garlic-themed cooking class as a savory start to spring.

Per serving

Calories 683
Fat 51 g
Cholesterol 119 mg
Sodium 1175 mg
Carbohydrate 33 g
Fiber 4 g

Rosemary Focaccia

Focaccia, Italy's famous flatbread, is crisp on the outside and slightly chewy on the inside. Try serving it warm with a little extra olive oil for dipping.

What Is Focaccia?

Focaccia is a traditional Italian yeast bread served as a snack, an appetizer, or as a sandwich bread. It's generally shaped into a flattened round loaf, brushed with olive oil, and sprinkled with salt and herbs. Dress it up with additional toppings like pesto, sun-dried tomatoes, or poppy seeds.

3 cups flour
1 envelope (2$1/4$ teaspoons) fast rising dry yeast
$1/2$ teaspoon salt
1 cup warm (115° to 125°F) water
4 tablespoons olive oil (divided)
$1/4$ cup grated asiago cheese
1 tablespoon chopped fresh rosemary
$1/4$ teaspoon coarse salt

In work bowl of food processor fitted with steel knife blade, combine flour, yeast, and the $1/2$ teaspoon salt. With machine running, pour water and 2 tablespoons of the olive oil through feed tube in slow steady stream; process until dough forms a ball. Let dough rest in processor bowl for 15 to 30 minutes. On lightly floured surface, roll dough into $1/2$-inch-thick round. Place on pizza pan that has been coated with no-stick cooking spray. Press fingertips into dough to form dimples. Drizzle remaining 2 tablespoons olive oil over dough. Sprinkle with cheese, rosemary, and coarse salt. Bake in 400°F oven until golden brown, about 15 to 18 minutes. Cut into wedges.

Makes 6-8 servings

Per serving

Calories 246
Fat 8 g
Cholesterol 3 mg
Sodium 249 mg
Carbohydrate 36 g
Fiber 2 g

Photograph on page 52

Piece-Of-Cake Cornbread

A square of this moist, tender, and sweet cornbread—warm from the oven—turns a bowl of soup or chili into a feast. Keep the ingredients on hand and make it anytime.

1 package (9 ounces) yellow
    cake mix
1 package (8½ ounces) corn
    muffin mix
2 eggs
1 cup milk
Honey butter (optional)

In large bowl, stir together mixes. In medium bowl, beat together eggs and milk. Add to mixes and stir until just combined. Pour into 8-inch square baking pan that has been coated with no-stick cooking spray. Bake in 400°F oven until wooden pick inserted in center comes out clean, about 30 minutes. If desired, serve with honey butter.

Makes 9 servings

Quick Breads

Recipes for quick breads and muffins direct you to mix dry and wet ingredients just until combined. For perfect breads, mix enough to incorporate all the flour, but do not beat. A few lumps in the batter are fine. In fact, overmixing causes tunnels, peaks, and an undesirable coarse texture.

Per serving

Calories 258
Fat 7 g
Cholesterol 50 mg
Sodium 513 mg
Carbohydrate 43 g
Fiber 2 g

Ham and Cheese Scones

Light and tender scones are a special treat. Studded with ham and cheese, these are terrific with a bowl of hot soup.

2 cups flour

1 tablespoon baking powder

1 1/2 teaspoons dried dill weed

1/2 teaspoon salt

1/8 teaspoon ground white pepper

4 tablespoons butter, chilled and
    cut into small pieces

1 1/2 cups diced ham

4 ounces (1 cup) finely shredded
    cheddar cheese

2 eggs

1/2 cup buttermilk

1 tablespoon butter, melted

In large bowl, whisk together flour, baking powder, dill, salt, and pepper. Using pastry blender or fork, cut in the 4 tablespoons butter until mixture resembles coarse meal. Stir in ham and cheese. In small bowl, whisk together eggs and buttermilk. Make well in center of flour mixture. Pour in egg mixture; stir with fork until dough forms ball. Gather dough into ball. Turn out onto lightly floured board and knead until smooth, about 10 times. Divide dough in half. Pat out each portion into 6 1/2-inch round, about 3/4-inch thick. Place on parchment-lined baking sheet. With knife, score each round into 6 wedges. Brush with melted butter. Bake in 400°F oven until lightly browned, about 20 to 25 minutes. Cut apart along score lines.

Makes 12 scones

ingredient savvy

Buttermilk

Buttermilk is used in scones, pancakes, or waffles to make them light and fluffy, and adds a slightly tangy flavor. As a bonus, all buttermilk is low-fat! If you don't have buttermilk on hand, pour one tablespoon vinegar or lemon juice into a liquid measuring cup. Add milk to total one cup. Stir and let stand five minutes before using.

Per scone

Calories 206

Fat 11 g

Cholesterol 69 mg

Sodium 556 mg

Carbohydrate 17 g

Fiber 1 g

Last-Minute Breads

No time to bake from scratch? No problem! Add a few special touches to refrigerated dough or a purchased loaf for fresh-baked flavor in minutes.

Parmesan Rolls

12 frozen white dough rolls
3 tablespoons grated parmesan
  cheese
1/4 teaspoon dried basil
2 tablespoons butter, melted

Thaw dough according to package directions using microwave-thaw method. In small bowl, combine parmesan and basil. Dip each roll into melted butter, then into cheese mixture. Place on parchment-lined baking sheet; cover with greased plastic wrap. Let rise at room temperature for 1 to 2 hours. Bake in 350°F oven until golden brown, about 8 to 10 minutes.

Makes 12 rolls

Sesame Twists

1 can (11 ounces) refrigerated soft
  bread sticks
2 tablespoons butter or margarine,
  melted
2 tablespoons sesame seed

Remove bread sticks from can; separate into 12 portions. Place on parchment-lined baking sheet. Brush tops with melted butter and sprinkle with sesame seed. Twist each stick twice, and press ends onto baking sheet. Bake in 375°F oven until golden brown, about 10 to 12 minutes.

Makes 12 bread sticks

Herbed Garlic Bread

1/2 cup mayonnaise
1 tablespoon dried chives
1 large clove garlic, minced
French baguette, cut into 1/2-inch
    thick slices

In small bowl, combine mayonnaise, chives, and garlic; set aside. Place 12 bread slices on foil-lined baking sheet; broil until toasted, about 1 minute. Turn each slice over. Spread mayonnaise mixture over untoasted sides of bread. Broil until lightly browned, about 1 to 2 minutes.

Makes 12 slices

Per slice

Calories 79
Fat 7 g
Cholesterol 4 mg
Sodium 78 mg
Carbohydrate 3 g
Fiber <1 g

Cheese Topped Bread

1 loaf (8 ounces) Italian bread
1/4 cup butter or margarine
2 teaspoons dried parsley flakes
1/4 teaspoon garlic powder
4 ounces (1 cup) shredded
    mozzarella cheese
1/2 cup grated romano cheese
1/2 cup grated parmesan cheese

Cut bread in half lengthwise; set aside. In small saucepan, melt butter; remove pan from heat. Stir in parsley and garlic powder. Brush over cut surfaces of bread. In small bowl, combine mozzarella, romano, and parmesan. Sprinkle over bread. Place bread on foil-lined baking sheet. Bake in 375°F oven until lightly browned, about 10 to 15 minutes. Cut each half into 8 slices.

Makes 8 servings

Per serving

Calories 210
Fat 13 g
Cholesterol 33 mg
Sodium 435 mg
Carbohydrate 16 g
Fiber 1 g

delicious, easy weeknight meals

What's for Dinner?

Quick Eggplant Parmesan

Everyone will love the layers of crispy "oven-fried" eggplant slices, gooey cheese, and tangy spaghetti sauce in this simplified Italian classic. Team it with a crisp Caesar salad and hot cooked spaghetti to catch the extra sauce.

1 eggplant (about 1 pound)
1 egg, beaten with
   1 tablespoon water
1 cup Italian seasoned bread crumbs
No-stick cooking spray
2 cups prepared spaghetti sauce
   (divided)
4 ounces (1 cup) shredded Italian
   cheese blend
Grated parmesan cheese (optional)

Trim eggplant; peel if desired. Cut eggplant into 1/4-inch thick slices. Dip slices in egg mixture; coat with bread crumbs. Place on foil-lined baking sheet. Lightly coat both sides of slices with cooking spray. Bake in 400°F oven until light brown, about 4 minutes per side. Arrange half of the slices in 8-inch square baking dish that has been coated with cooking spray. Top with 1 cup of the sauce. Add remaining slices and sauce; top with cheese. Bake in 400°F oven until sauce is bubbly and cheese melts, about 15 to 20 minutes. Sprinkle parmesan cheese over the top.

Makes 4 servings

Per serving

Calories 301
Fat 10 g
Cholesterol 73 mg
Sodium 1604 mg
Carbohydrate 42 g
Fiber 7 g

Ravioli Lasagna

It's easy to keep all the ingredients on hand for this irresistible Italian feast. Add a crisp garden salad and some warm bread sticks for a hearty, no-fuss meal.

1 package (25 ounces) frozen beef or
   cheese ravioli
1 container (15 ounces)
   ricotta cheese
1 package (10 ounces) frozen
   chopped spinach, thawed and
   well drained
1 egg, slightly beaten
1 teaspoon dried basil
1 jar (26 to 30 ounces) prepared
   spaghetti sauce
4 ounces (1 cup) shredded
   mozzarella cheese
3/4 cup grated parmesan or
   asiago cheese

Cook ravioli according to package directions. Drain; set aside. In small bowl, combine ricotta cheese, spinach, egg, and basil. Spread 1 cup of the sauce in 9×13-inch baking dish that has been lightly coated with no-stick cooking spray. Arrange half of the cooked ravioli in single layer. Place dollops of ricotta mixture over ravioli layer; gently spread to make even layer. Sprinkle mozzarella over ricotta mixture. Top with remaining ravioli and sauce. Cover and bake in 350°F oven until sauce is bubbly, about 30 to 35 minutes. Sprinkle parmesan over top. Bake uncovered for 5 minutes. Let stand for 10 minutes before serving.

Makes 6 servings

technique savvy

Cooking for a Few

Don't let cooking just for two or a few keep you from enjoying your favorite casseroles! When assembling the recipe, divide the ingredients between two smaller pans. Bake one now and freeze the other. Cover the casserole tightly with heavy-duty aluminum foil and freeze for up to one month. What a great way to have dinner on hand!

Per serving

Calories 413
Fat 19 g
Cholesterol 80 mg
Sodium 1597 mg
Carbohydrate 38 g
Fiber 5 g

Asparagus Fettuccine Alfredo

One pot is all you need to make this rich, creamy pasta flavored with tender asparagus and mushrooms. Serve it with spring greens drizzled with balsamic vinaigrette and a basket of crusty bread.

technique savvy

Al Dente Pasta

Start with a large pot of water at a rolling boil to give pasta plenty of room. Stir the pasta occasionally to keep it separated. Cook only until *al dente*—just until tender *to the tooth*—to keep it from getting gummy.

Don't add oil to the cooking water, which will prevent the sauce from clinging to the pasta.

2^1/$_2$ cups water
1 teaspoon salt
8 ounces fettuccine, broken
    into fourths
1 pound asparagus, trimmed and
    cut into bite-sized pieces
1 cup heavy whipping cream
^{1}/$_2$ pound sliced mushrooms
^{1}/$_4$ cup thinly sliced green onion
1 large clove garlic, minced
^{1}/$_4$ teaspoon ground white pepper
^{1}/$_2$ cup grated parmesan cheese

In 3-quart saucepan, bring water and salt to a boil over high heat. Stir in fettuccine; cover loosely and adjust heat to boil gently for 5 minutes, stirring occasionally. Add asparagus, and cook stirring occasionally until most of the water has been absorbed, about 5 minutes. Add cream, mushrooms, green onion, garlic, and pepper. Cook over medium heat, stirring frequently until creamy, about 8 to 10 minutes. Toss in parmesan cheese.

Makes 4 servings

Per serving

Calories 369
Fat 28 g
Cholesterol 112 mg
Sodium 776 mg
Carbohydrate 21 g
Fiber 2 g

Bowties with Chicken & Mushrooms in Garlic Sauce

Porcini and shiitake mushrooms add a wonderful earthy flavor to this elegant dish that's perfect for last-minute guests. Serve steamed broccoli alongside.

1 package (1/2 ounce) dried porcini mushrooms
8 ounces bowtie pasta
2 tablespoons butter
1/2 pound boneless, skinless chicken breast halves, cut into 1-inch pieces
1/2 pound shiitake mushrooms, stemmed and caps sliced
1 shallot, diced
3 cloves garlic, minced
1 cup heavy whipping cream
1 cup chicken broth
1 teaspoon Cajun/Creole seasoning
1/4 teaspoon ground white pepper

In 1-cup glass measure, soak porcini mushrooms in 1/2 cup hot water for 20 minutes (do not drain). In large pot of rapidly boiling water, cook pasta for 6 minutes; drain and set aside. In large saucepan, melt butter over medium-high heat. Add chicken and cook, stirring frequently until no longer pink, about 2 to 3 minutes. Remove chicken from pan. Add shiitake mushrooms, shallot, and garlic; cook for 1 to 2 minutes. Stir in porcini mushrooms with liquid and remaining ingredients. Add drained pasta. Bring to a boil over medium heat; cook until pasta is tender, about 6 to 8 minutes. Add chicken and cook until chicken is heated through, about 1 to 2 minutes.

Makes 4-6 servings

Per serving

Calories 422
Fat 20 g
Cholesterol 80 mg
Sodium 421 mg
Carbohydrate 33 g
Fiber 1 g

Easy Chicken Gumbo

Freshly baked cornbread is the perfect partner to this quick version of a Creole favorite. Keep the hot pepper sauce handy for those who want a little extra zip.

2 tablespoons vegetable oil

1 pound boneless, skinless
    chicken breast halves,
    cut into bite-sized pieces

1 teaspoon Old Bay seasoning

2 tablespoons flour

1/2 pound smoked sausage, sliced
    (optional)

2 cans (14 1/2 ounces each)
    stewed tomatoes

2 1/3 cups (1/2 of 16-ounce package)
    frozen okra, thawed

1 cup coarsely chopped mushrooms

1 teaspoon hot pepper sauce

6 cups hot cooked rice

In medium saucepan, heat oil over medium-high heat. Add chicken; sprinkle Old Bay seasoning over chicken. Cook, stirring frequently until chicken is no longer pink, about 3 to 4 minutes. Sprinkle flour over chicken; cook, stirring frequently for 2 minutes. Stir in sausage, tomatoes, okra, mushrooms, and hot sauce. Bring to a boil; reduce heat and simmer until heated through, about 8 minutes. Serve over rice.

Makes 4-6 servings

TIP One pound peeled and deveined medium shrimp may be substituted for chicken.

ingredient savvy

Fresh Okra

Okra, a popular vegetable in the South, is perhaps best known as a staple ingredient in gumbo. It not only adds color and flavor, it also helps thicken the spicy stew. Purchase okra either fresh or frozen. Fresh okra should have small pods that are bright green. Larger pods can be tough.

Per serving

Calories 382

Fat 6 g

Cholesterol 29 mg

Sodium 572 mg

Carbohydrate 63 g

Fiber 4 g

Country French Pot Pies

Filled with plenty of chicken, colorful vegetables, and a sprinkle of fragrant herbs, these cozy and comforting pot pies are a complete meal. Refrigerated pie crust makes them so simple to prepare. Add a tossed salad to round out the meal.

ingredient savvy

Herbes de Provence

Herbes de Provence is a blend of dried herbs used in the cuisine of the Provence region of southern France. A typical blend might include basil, fennel, lavender, marjoram, rosemary, sage, summer savory, and thyme. Sprinkle herbes de Provence over roasted chicken or beef, or use it to season other meat or vegetable dishes.

2 tablespoons butter
1 cup sliced mushrooms
    (about 4 ounces)
1 teaspoon herbes de Provence
1 large Yukon gold, russet, or butter
    potato, cubed (about 1 cup)
1 large sweet potato, peeled and
    cubed (about 1 cup)
3 tablespoons flour
1 can (14 ounces) chicken broth
1 cup shredded cooked chicken
1/2 cup frozen peas
1 refrigerated pie crust (1/2 of
    15-ounce package)

In large skillet, melt butter over medium-high heat. Add mushrooms and herbs; cook until most liquid is absorbed, about 5 minutes. Add potatoes; cook for 5 minutes, stirring occasionally. Stir in flour. Add broth; bring to a boil. Reduce heat and simmer until potatoes are tender and mixture is thickened, about 5 minutes. Stir in chicken and peas. Divide mixture evenly among four 10-ounce custard cups. On lightly floured surface, unfold pie crust. Cut 4 rounds slightly larger than top of custard cups. Place over top of filling. Pierce crust several times. Place on foil-lined baking sheet. Bake in 400°F oven until crust is golden, about 18 to 20 minutes.

Makes 4 servings

Per serving

Calories 462
Fat 24 g
Cholesterol 59 mg
Sodium 728 mg
Carbohydrate 46 g
Fiber 3 g

Weeknight Cashew Chicken

A crisp, colorful stir-fry is a great one-dish meal for a busy weeknight. Have all the ingredients chopped and measured before you start—this cooks quickly! Finish off your meal with fortune cookies.

1 pound boneless, skinless
  chicken breast halves
1 cup chicken broth
1 tablespoon cornstarch
2 tablespoons soy sauce
2 large cloves garlic, minced
2 tablespoons vegetable oil
1/2 pound broccoli, coarsely
  chopped
1/2 red or green bell pepper,
  cut into 1/2-inch pieces
5 green onions, sliced diagonally
  into 1-inch pieces
Hot cooked Chinese noodles or rice
1/2 cup cashews, toasted

Cut chicken into bite-sized pieces; set aside. In 2-cup measure, combine broth, cornstarch, soy sauce, and garlic. Heat wok or large nonstick skillet over medium-high heat. Add oil, chicken, broccoli, and bell pepper; stir-fry until chicken is cooked through, about 3 to 5 minutes. Stir broth mixture into center of wok; cook, stirring constantly until thickened. Stir in green onions; stir-fry for 1 minute. Serve over Chinese noodles or rice. Sprinkle cashews over top.

Makes 4 servings

ingredient savvy

Asian Noodles

Noodles symbolize long life and are an important part of Asian cuisine and culture. The varieties differ from one country to another and are made from any number of ingredients, including wheat, rice, soy, and buckwheat. Cook in plenty of boiling water just until they are tender to prevent sticky, gummy noodles.

Per serving without noodles or rice

Calories 280
Fat 16 g
Cholesterol 43 mg
Sodium 771 mg
Carbohydrate 13 g
Fiber 2 g

Chicken Piccata

Tender chicken with a light lemon sauce is an Italian classic. Serve it with delicate angel hair pasta.

cuisine savvy

What Is Piccata?

Piccata, a classic Italian dish, may be made with medallions of chicken or veal. Flatten chicken breasts prior to sautéing for quick, even cooking. The delicate flavor of its distinguishing sauce, made with pan drippings, is enhanced by the addition of lemon juice, white wine, and chopped parsley.

4 boneless, skinless
    chicken breast halves
1/4 cup flour
1 1/2 teaspoons Italian herb seasoning
2 tablespoons olive oil
1 cup chicken broth
1 clove garlic, minced
1/4 teaspoon salt
2 tablespoons fresh lemon juice
Chopped fresh Italian parsley

Place chicken between 2 sheets of plastic wrap; pound lightly to even thickness. In shallow dish, combine flour and Italian seasoning. Coat chicken in flour mixture; set aside remaining flour. In medium skillet, heat oil over medium-high heat. Add chicken and cook until browned and juices run clear, about 4 to 5 minutes per side. Remove from skillet; cover to keep warm. Stir chicken broth into skillet; bring to a boil over medium-high heat. Stir in garlic and salt. In small bowl, whisk together lemon juice and reserved seasoned flour. Stir into chicken broth; cook until thickened, about 2 to 3 minutes. Spoon over chicken and garnish with parsley.

Makes 4 servings

TIP If desired, white wine may be substituted for up to half of the chicken broth.

Per serving

Calories 176
Fat 8 g
Cholesterol 43 mg
Sodium 439 mg
Carbohydrate 7 g
Fiber <1 g

Margarita Fish Bake

Kissed with a tangy citrus glaze, this mild white fish is an easy entrée the whole family will love. Serve with steamed baby carrots tossed with butter and a drizzle of honey.

1¹⁄₂ pounds tilapia or orange
    roughy fillets
1 teaspoon grated lime peel
2 tablespoons fresh lime juice
2 tablespoons orange marmalade
2 tablespoons tequila or orange juice
Few drops hot pepper sauce
Coarse salt

Rinse fish and pat dry. In 9×13-inch baking dish, combine remaining ingredients except salt. Place fish in baking dish; turn to coat. Fold under thin ends, if needed. Bake in 425°F oven until fish flakes easily with fork, about 10 to 12 minutes. Season lightly with salt.

Makes 6 servings

Santa Fe Fillets

Catfish goes "crunch" with a crispy coating of crushed tortilla chips. A salad of shredded lettuce, diced cucumbers, and tomatoes makes a great side dish.

1 pound catfish or orange
    roughy fillets
1 cup finely crushed tortilla chips
1 teaspoon chili powder
¹⁄₂ cup plain yogurt or buttermilk
Salsa

Rinse fish and pat dry. In shallow dish, combine crushed chips and chili powder. Brush fish with yogurt. Roll fish in chip mixture to coat. Place fish on foil-lined baking sheet. Bake in 425°F oven until fish flakes easily with fork, about 10 to 12 minutes. Serve with salsa.

Makes 4 servings

contributed by

Karen Hurych

Staff Home Economist Karen Hurych joined Dierbergs School of Cooking in 1989. Karen inherited her love of cooking, baking, and home-canning from both her mother and grandmother. As Test Kitchen Manager, she final-tests all of the recipes that appear on Dierbergs recipe cards, *Everybody Cooks®* magazine and *Dierbergs Presents Everybody Cooks®* television show, and is the prop stylist for these projects. Karen also develops recipes for the Eat Hearty® cooking classes she co-teaches with registered dietitians from Missouri Baptist Medical Center.

Per serving fillets

Calories 281
Fat 15 g
Cholesterol 55 mg
Sodium 201 mg
Carbohydrate 16 g
Fiber 2 g

Per serving fish bake

Calories 71
Fat 1 g
Cholesterol 0 mg
Sodium 28 mg
Carbohydrate 6 g
Fiber <1 g

Lemon Crumb Tilapia

Everyone will love these mild, crispy fillets with a hint of lemon. To complete your meal, add a steamed green vegetable and some fresh-from-the-oven cornbread.

ingredient savvy

Tilapia

Tilapia is a flaky white-fleshed fish that is available fresh and frozen. To thaw, immerse an unopened package of frozen fillets in cold water for about 30 minutes. Fresh tilapia fillets are typically thicker and take longer to cook. Tilapia has a mild flavor, making it suitable for any recipe calling for white fish such as sole or orange roughy.

1 pound tilapia fillets
1/4 cup Italian seasoned bread crumbs
2 tablespoons grated parmesan cheese
1 teaspoon garlic salt
1 teaspoon grated lemon peel
3 tablespoons butter (divided)
1 tablespoon vegetable oil
2 tablespoons fresh lemon juice

Cut fillets in half lengthwise. In shallow dish, combine bread crumbs, parmesan, garlic salt, and lemon peel. Place 2 tablespoons of the butter in glass pie plate. Microwave (high) for 30 seconds. Dip fillets in melted butter; coat with crumb mixture. In large nonstick skillet, melt remaining 1 tablespoon butter with oil over medium-high heat. Add fillets and cook until fish flakes easily with fork, about 2 to 4 minutes per side. Sprinkle lemon juice over fish.

Makes 4 servings

Per serving

Calories 259
Fat 17 g
Cholesterol 26 mg
Sodium 505 mg
Carbohydrate 7 g
Fiber <1 g

Spicy Cajun Shrimp

Packed with flavor, these lively shrimp are spiced just right. Add mixed bean salad or crisp cole slaw for a deliciously cool accompaniment.

Cajun or Creole?

Despite their many similarities, Cajun and Creole cuisines are distinctly different. A blend of French and Southern cooking, Cajun cooking is hearty, spicy, home-style food. Creole dishes are typically more refined, using lots of tomatoes, butter, and cream.

1 pound medium shrimp
3 tablespoons butter or margarine
2 cloves garlic, minced
1 teaspoon Worcestershire sauce
2 teaspoons Cajun/Creole seasoning
1 1/2 teaspoons Italian herb seasoning
1 large tomato, chopped
1/4 cup beer, at room temperature
3 cups hot cooked rice

Peel and devein shrimp; set aside. In large skillet, cook butter, garlic, Worcestershire sauce, and seasonings over high heat until butter is melted. Add shrimp and tomato; cook, stirring frequently until shrimp are opaque, about 2 minutes. Add beer; cover and cook for 1 minute. Serve over rice.

Makes 3 servings

TIP If desired, substitute 1/2 cup canned diced tomatoes for fresh tomato.

Per serving

Calories 513
Fat 15 g
Cholesterol 262 mg
Sodium 1109 mg
Carbohydrate 54 g
Fiber 2 g

Rush Hour Swiss Steak

Old-fashioned flavor doesn't have to take all day. This streamlined favorite and its flavorful sauce is terrific with mashed potatoes or buttered egg noodles.

2 pounds lean ground beef
3 tablespoons flour
1/2 teaspoon salt
1/4 teaspoon ground black pepper
1 tablespoon vegetable oil
1 cup chopped onion
1 can (14 1/2 ounces) diced or stewed Italian-style tomatoes
1/2 cup dry red wine or beef broth

Shape beef into 6 patties. On sheet of waxed paper, combine flour, salt, and pepper. Coat both sides of patties in flour mixture, shaking off excess. Reserve remaining flour mixture. In large nonstick skillet, heat oil over medium-high heat. Add beef patties; cook until browned, about 5 minutes per side. (If necessary, cook in 2 batches.) Transfer beef to plate; cover to keep warm. Add onion to skillet and stir to scrape browned bits from bottom of skillet; cook until onion is soft, about 5 minutes. Stir in reserved flour mixture; cook for 1 minute. Stir in tomatoes and wine. Add beef; cover and simmer, stirring sauce occasionally, until internal temperature is 160°F, about 15 minutes.

Makes 6 servings

Per serving

Calories 401
Fat 25 g
Cholesterol 101 mg
Sodium 588 mg
Carbohydrate 9 g
Fiber 1 g

Classic Meat Loaf with Horseradish Sauce

A blend of ground beef and pork makes this meatloaf moist and flavorful. The lively horseradish sauce adds a little extra zip. Mashed potatoes are the perfect accompaniment.

2 eggs

1 can (6 ounces) tomato paste

1 cup finely chopped onion

1/2 cup old-fashioned or
    quick-cooking rolled oats

2 tablespoons soy sauce

1 teaspoon salt

1/2 teaspoon ground black pepper

1 pound lean ground beef

1/2 pound ground pork

1/3 cup chili sauce or ketchup

Horseradish Sauce (recipe follows)

In large bowl, combine eggs, tomato paste, onion, oats, soy sauce, salt, and pepper; mix well. Crumble beef and pork into bowl. Mix until combined. (Do not overmix.) Press mixture into 9×5-inch loaf pan that has been coated with no-stick cooking spray. Spread chili sauce over top. Bake in 350°F oven until internal temperature is 165°F, about 1 to 1 1/4 hours. Let rest in pan for 15 minutes. Turn out onto serving platter; cut into thick slices. Serve with Horseradish Sauce.

Makes 6 servings

Horseradish Sauce

1/2 cup mayonnaise

1/2 cup dairy sour cream

2 cloves garlic, minced

2 tablespoons prepared horseradish

1 tablespoon minced fresh parsley

Dash ground white pepper

In small bowl, combine all ingredients; stir to blend. Cover and refrigerate several hours or up to 3 days to blend flavors.

Makes 1 cup

Horseradish

Did you know that most of the world's horseradish is grown near Collinsville, Illinois? This ancient herb has been used for medicinal purposes and as an aphrodisiac, but is best known for the familiar zip it adds to recipes. Prepared horseradish loses its pungency over time, so purchase it in small quantities. Refrigerate the jar, tightly closed and upside-down, to keep air out and flavor in.

**Per serving with
2 tablespoons sauce**

Calories 424

Fat 24 g

Cholesterol 158 mg

Sodium 1534 mg

Carbohydrate 19 g

Fiber 3 g

Moo Shu Beef

Marinate steak and stir-fry with convenient slaw mix and pre-sliced mushrooms. Then wrap, roll, and you're ready to eat! Serve with a salad of fresh tropical fruit.

ingredient savvy

Fresh Ginger

Fresh ginger adds a sweet, spicy bite to your dish. Use a teaspoon to scrape off the thin, beige skin, then slice or mince. The smaller the pieces, the more pungent the flavor will be. Wrap leftover ginger in plastic wrap and store in the refrigerator for several weeks, or freeze for up to 6 months.

2 tablespoon low sodium soy sauce
2 tablespoons water
2 cloves garlic, minced
1 tablespoon grated fresh
    ginger root
1 tablespoon cornstarch
2 teaspoons sugar
1 pound boneless beef sirloin,
    sliced into thin strips
1 teaspoon vegetable oil
1 teaspoon grated fresh ginger root
3 cups prepared slaw mix
    (about 6 ounces)
1 package (8 ounces) sliced
    mushrooms
1/2 cup sliced green onion
2 tablespoons hoisin sauce
8 large flour tortillas
    (8-inch diameter)

In large reclosable freezer-weight plastic bag, combine soy sauce, water, garlic, the 1 tablespoon ginger, cornstarch, and sugar. Add beef; seal bag and toss to coat. Place bag on plate and marinate in refrigerator for 2 to 4 hours. In wok or large nonstick skillet, heat oil over medium-high heat. Add the 1 teaspoon ginger; stir-fry for 30 seconds. Remove beef from bag; discard marinade. Add beef to wok; stir-fry for 2 minutes. Add slaw mix, mushrooms, and green onion; cover and cook for 2 minutes, stirring occasionally. Spread hoisin sauce over tortillas. Divide beef mixture among tortillas; roll up burrito-style.

Makes 4 servings

Per serving

Calories 522
Fat 13 g
Cholesterol 102 mg
Sodium 481 mg
Carbohydrate 57 g
Fiber 4 g

French Onion Skillet Chops

For tender pork chops every time, cook them quickly to an internal temperature of 155°F. You'll want mashed potatoes on the side to capture every bite of the delicious onion gravy.

4 boneless pork loin chops
   (about 1 pound), trimmed

Salt and pepper to taste

1 tablespoon vegetable oil

1 medium onion, sliced

2 cloves garlic, slivered

1 can (14 ounces) beef broth
   (divided)

1/4 cup dry white wine (optional)

1 teaspoon Worcestershire sauce

3 tablespoons flour

Season both sides of pork with salt and pepper. In large nonstick skillet, heat oil over medium-high heat. Add onion; cover and cook, stirring occasionally until softened, about 2 to 3 minutes. Uncover and cook until golden brown, about 3 minutes. Add garlic. Push onion and garlic to sides of pan. Add pork; cook until browned, about 2 to 3 minutes per side. Reserve 1/2 cup of the broth. Add remaining broth, wine, and Worcestershire sauce to skillet; bring to a boil. Reduce heat, cover, and simmer until pork is tender and internal temperature is 155°F, about 5 to 7 minutes. Transfer meat to platter. Stir flour into reserved broth. Bring liquid in pan to a boil over medium-high heat. Slowly whisk in flour mixture. Cook, whisking frequently until thickened, about 1 to 2 minutes.

Makes 4 servings

Tender, Juicy Pork

Today's pork is very lean and the secret to making it tender is to cook it quickly. Pork is food safe when the center is still pink. Remove it from the heat when the internal temperature reaches 150°F, tent loosely with foil, and let stand five to ten minutes. As it rests, the internal temperature will rise to 155°F. Your pork will be tender, juicy, and perfectly cooked.

Per serving

Calories 205

Fat 9 g

Cholesterol 50 mg

Sodium 423 mg

Carbohydrate 8 g

Fiber 1 g

to complete your meal

Salads and Side Dishes

Crumbled Blue Cheese Dressing

Drizzle over tender Bibb lettuce, glazed pecans, and dried cherries or cranberries.

1/4 cup extra virgin olive oil

3 tablespoons red wine vinegar

1 tablespoon sugar

2 teaspoons dijon-style mustard

3 ounces blue cheese, crumbled

In screw-top jar, combine all ingredients except blue cheese. Shake vigorously to blend. Toss greens with dressing; sprinkle crumbled cheese over top.

Makes about 1/2 cup

Mayfair Dressing

Serve this zesty St. Louis classic over crisp salad greens, such as iceberg or romaine.

1 cup mayonnaise

2 tablespoons finely chopped onion

2 tablespoons finely chopped celery

1 tablespoon horseradish mustard

2 teaspoons anchovy paste

1/2 teaspoon coarsely ground
   black pepper

In small bowl, stir together all ingredients until well blended.

Makes about 1 cup

Dressing Salads

Preparing salad ingredients ahead of time saves a lot of last-minute fuss. Be sure to store them in separate containers and combine just before serving. Salad dressing may be made ahead and refrigerated in a tightly covered container. Shake well and drizzle over salad, toss to coat, and serve immediately.

**Per 2 tablespoons
Blue Cheese Dressing**

Calories 209

Fat 20 g

Cholesterol 16 mg

Sodium 311 mg

Carbohydrate 4 g

Fiber 0 g

**Per 2 tablespoons
Mayfair Dressing**

Calories 202

Fat 22 g

Cholesterol 15 mg

Sodium 282 mg

Carbohydrate 2 g

Fiber <1 g

Lemon Greek Vinaigrette

Toss with crisp iceberg lettuce, ripe olives, cucumbers, grape tomatoes, and feta cheese. Add strips of grilled chicken breast to make it a main dish.

1/3 cup extra virgin olive oil

2 teaspoons grated lemon peel

1/4 cup fresh lemon juice

1/2 teaspoon dried oregano, crushed

1/4 teaspoon garlic salt

1/4 teaspoon ground black pepper

In small bowl, whisk together all ingredients until well blended.

Makes about 1/2 cup

Balsamic Vinaigrette

Toss with tender field greens, fresh berries, mandarin oranges, and toasted sliced almonds.

1/4 cup balsamic vinegar

1 tablespoon honey

1 clove garlic, minced

1/4 teaspoon ground black pepper

1/4 teaspoon dried oregano, crushed

1/8 teaspoon salt

2 tablespoons extra virgin olive oil

In small bowl, whisk together all ingredients except oil. Whisking vigorously, add oil in slow steady stream until well blended.

Makes about 1/2 cup

Extra Virgin Olive Oil

Extra virgin olive oil comes from the first pressing of the olives. Prized for its low acidity and fruity flavor, the color of extra virgin olive oil ranges from almost clear to bright green. Generally, the deeper the color of the oil, the more pronounced the flavor. Use extra virgin olive oil in salad dressings and other recipes in which you want its distinct flavor.

Per 2 tablespoons Greek Vinaigrette

Calories 162

Fat 18 g

Cholesterol 0 mg

Sodium 61 mg

Carbohydrate 2 g

Fiber <1 g

Per 2 tablespoons Balsamic Vinaigrette

Calories 87

Fat 7 g

Cholesterol 0 mg

Sodium 73 mg

Carbohydrate 8 g

Fiber <1 g

Strawberry Gouda Spinach Salad

The slightly nutty flavor of gouda cheese blends beautifully with juicy berries and grapes in this luscious salad. It's a delicious accompaniment to grilled chicken or pork.

6 ounces (6 cups) fresh baby
    spinach
2 cups sliced strawberries
1 cup halved seedless red grapes
1/4 cup thinly sliced sweet onion
    (Maui, Vidalia, or red)
7 ounces gouda cheese, cubed
    (about 1 cup)
Poppy Seed Dressing (recipe
    follows)
Sugared Almonds (recipe follows)

Rinse spinach; spin or pat dry. In large salad bowl, combine spinach, strawberries, grapes, onion, and gouda. Drizzle dressing over salad; toss to coat. Top with almonds.

Makes 6 servings

Poppy Seed Dressing

1/4 cup vegetable oil
3 tablespoons white wine vinegar
2 tablespoons minced shallot
2 tablespoons sugar
2 teaspoons poppy seed
1/4 teaspoon dry mustard

In small bowl, whisk together all ingredients until well blended.

Makes about 1/2 cup

Sugared Almonds

In small heavy skillet, cook 1/3 cup almonds and 3 tablespoons sugar over medium heat, stirring constantly, until sugar melts and almonds are lightly toasted, about 5 minutes. Spread on parchment paper to cool. Break apart, if needed. Store in airtight container. Makes 1/3 cup

Per serving with dressing and almonds

Calories 339
Fat 23 g
Cholesterol 37 mg
Sodium 304 mg
Carbohydrate 24 g
Fiber 3 g

Boston Lettuce Salad with Cranberry Vinaigrette

Crisping Greens

For crisp salads, wash and dry greens in a salad spinner. Roll them gently in paper towels and refrigerate for several hours. For longer storage, place in a plastic bag and refrigerate. Greens will stay fresh for five to seven days.

8 cups torn Boston and/or Bibb lettuce
1/2 cup sliced green onion
Cranberry Vinaigrette (recipe follows)
1 can (11 ounces) mandarin oranges, drained
1/2 cup sweetened dried cranberries
1/2 cup Glazed Pecans (recipe follows)

In large bowl, combine greens and green onion. Drizzle dressing over salad; toss to coat. Place on individual serving plates. Sprinkle oranges, cranberries, and pecans over top of each salad.

Makes 6-8 servings

Cranberry Vinaigrette

1/4 cup cranberry juice cocktail
2 tablespoons vegetable oil
1 tablespoon honey
1 tablespoon red wine vinegar
1/2 teaspoon ground allspice
Salt and coarsely ground black pepper to taste

In small bowl, whisk together all ingredients until well blended.

Makes about 1/2 cup

Glazed Pecans

1/2 cup halved or coarsely chopped pecans
1/4 cup sugar

In small heavy skillet, cook pecans and sugar over medium heat, stirring constantly, until sugar melts and pecans are lightly toasted, about 5 minutes. Spread on parchment paper to cool. Break apart, if needed. Store in airtight container.

Makes 1/2 cup

Per serving with 1 tablespoon dressing

Calories 145
Fat 7 g
Cholesterol 0 mg
Sodium 6 mg
Carbohydrate 21 g
Fiber 2 g

Chipotle Apple Salad

Crisp, tart apples add a nice crunch to this flavorful salad. Chipotle chiles give the honey dressing a touch of smoky heat.

1 bag (8 ounces) European blend
    salad greens
3 Granny Smith apples, cored
    and cubed
1/2 cup sliced red onion
Chipotle Vinaigrette (recipe follows)
2 ounces (1/2 cup) crumbled
    feta cheese
1/4 pound thick-sliced bacon, cooked
    crisp and crumbled
1/3 cup slivered almonds, toasted

In large salad bowl, combine greens, apples, and onion. Drizzle dressing over top; toss to coat. Sprinkle feta, bacon, and almonds over top.

Makes 6 servings

Chipotle Vinaigrette

2 tablespoons cider vinegar
2 tablespoons honey
1 tablespoon olive oil
1 teaspoon pureed chipotle chiles
    in adobo sauce

In blender container, combine all ingredients. Blend for 30 seconds or until well mixed.

Makes 1/3 cup

TIP For information on chipotles, see sidebar on page 125.

contributed by

Pam Pahl

Home Economist Pam Pahl is the manager of the West Oak School of Cooking, with experience in nutrition, food service, and quantity cooking. Her culinary interest began at age three, when she would push a chair up to the stove to help stir whatever was in the pot. Her classes are friendly and relaxed, and she loves mixing lots of colors, flavors, and textures into her menus. While vegetarian cooking is her passion, her first love will always be dessert.

Per serving with dressing

Calories 216
Fat 12 g
Cholesterol 14 mg
Sodium 260 mg
Carbohydrate 20 g
Fiber 3 g

Pink Lemonade Fruit Salad

A tangy lemonade dressing makes a medley of summer fruits even more refreshing. It's the perfect take-along for your next picnic or barbecue.

4 cups melon balls or cubes
  (cantaloupe, honeydew, and/or
  watermelon)
2 cups seedless red or green grapes
2 cups strawberry halves
1 cup fresh blueberries
1/3 cup frozen pink lemonade
  concentrate, thawed
1 tablespoon sugar

Combine fruit in large non-metal bowl; set aside. In 1-cup glass measure, combine lemonade concentrate and sugar. Microwave (high) for 30 seconds. Stir to dissolve sugar. Pour over fruit; toss to coat. Cover and refrigerate for several hours.

Makes 8-10 servings

Per serving fruit salad

Calories 78
Fat <1 g
Cholesterol 0 mg
Sodium 9 mg
Carbohydrate 20 g
Fiber 2 g

Per serving tomatoes

Calories 127
Fat 10 g
Cholesterol 7 mg
Sodium 331 mg
Carbohydrate 9 g
Fiber 2 g

Tomatoes with Shallot Vinaigrette

Fresh, juicy, vine-ripened tomatoes—nothing else tastes quite like summer!

1 1/2 pounds tomatoes
  (about 6 medium), sliced
1 box (10 ounces) grape tomatoes,
  halved
1/4 cup minced shallots
1 clove garlic, minced
3 tablespoons extra virgin olive oil
2 tablespoons white balsamic or
  white wine vinegar
1/2 teaspoon salt
Coarsely ground black pepper
  to taste
2 ounces (1/2 cup) crumbled
  feta cheese
2 tablespoons slivered fresh basil

Arrange sliced tomatoes in single layer around edge of serving platter, overlapping slightly. Mound grape tomatoes in center. In small bowl, combine shallots, garlic, olive oil, vinegar, and salt; stir until well blended. Drizzle over tomatoes. Season with pepper, and sprinkle with feta and basil. Let stand 15 minutes before serving.

Makes 6 servings

TIP This salad is especially beautiful if you use a combination of red and yellow tomatoes.

Garden Risotto

Slow simmering and frequent stirring will reward you with rich, creamy risotto. Colorful vegetables, fragrant basil, and parmesan cheese make this version simply divine!

cuisine savvy

What Is Risotto?

Risotto is a creamy rice dish from Northern Italy that doesn't contain any cream at all. It's made with arborio rice, and cooked slowly to give it a rich, creamy consistency. The secret to great risotto is to cook it uncovered, stirring frequently, and adding warm broth a little at a time. Add cooked meat or seafood, vegetables, or cheeses, and serve risotto as an entrée or side dish.

2 cans (14 ounces each)
    chicken broth
1/3 cup dry white wine
2 tablespoons olive oil
2 tablespoons butter or margarine
1 cup arborio rice
1 small carrot, diced (about 1/2 cup)
1 small zucchini, diced
    (about 1/2 cup)
1/2 red or yellow bell pepper, diced
1/2 cup fresh asparagus tips
    (optional)
2 cloves garlic, minced
1/3 cup grated parmesan cheese
1 tablespoon chopped fresh basil,
    or 1 teaspoon dried

In medium saucepan, heat chicken broth and wine over medium heat. Reduce heat to keep broth hot but not boiling. In another medium saucepan, heat olive oil and butter over medium-high heat until butter melts. Add rice; cook, stirring constantly for 1 minute. Reduce heat to medium-low; add carrot and 1 cup of the hot broth. Cook, stirring frequently until most of the liquid is absorbed. Add another cup of hot broth. Continue to cook, stirring frequently until most of the liquid is absorbed, about 5 minutes. Add zucchini, bell pepper, asparagus, garlic, and remaining broth; cook until rice is tender and has very creamy texture, about 15 minutes. (Total cooking time is about 30 minutes.) Stir in parmesan and basil. Serve immediately.

Makes 4 servings

Per serving

Calories 342
Fat 16 g
Cholesterol 24 mg
Sodium 968 mg
Carbohydrate 43 g
Fiber 2 g

Photograph on page 150

Best-Ever Baked Beans

This colorful pot of beans has a rich, thick sauce with just the right balance of sweet and tart. Serve it alongside baked ham or, of course, at your next barbecue!

1/2 pound bacon, diced (9 slices)
1 large onion, chopped
3/4 cup firmly packed brown sugar
3/4 cup ketchup
1/4 cup cider vinegar
1 can (20 to 21 ounces) pork and
    beans in tomato sauce
1 can (15 to 16 ounces) navy beans,
    rinsed and drained
1 can (15 to 16 ounces) garbanzo
    beans (chick peas), rinsed
    and drained
1 can (15 to 16 ounces) black beans,
    rinsed and drained

In medium skillet over medium heat, cook bacon until crisp. Remove with slotted spoon and drain well on paper towels; set aside. In same skillet, cook onion in bacon drippings over medium heat, stirring frequently until tender, about 5 minutes. In deep 3-quart casserole, stir together brown sugar, ketchup, and vinegar. Add onion and all beans. Stir until well mixed. Cover and bake in 350°F oven until bubbly, about 1 hour. If desired, remove lid and cook for 5 minutes to thicken sauce. Sprinkle bacon over top.

Makes 16 servings

TIP If you are taking the beans to a picnic or barbecue, you can keep beans hot by wrapping the casserole completely in foil. Then wrap it in a clean terry cloth towel. Beans will stay hot for at least 1 hour.

Safe Food— Inside or Out

Whether you're dining inside or outdoors, don't let unfriendly bacteria spoil your feast. Keep hot foods hot—above 140°F—by placing them on the barbecue grill. Keep cold foods cold—below 40°F—by nestling salad bowls inside a larger bowl filled with ice. And play it safe with leftovers. Discard any food that's been sitting out longer than two hours.

Per serving

Calories 207
Fat 4 g
Cholesterol 8 mg
Sodium 508 mg
Carbohydrate 33 g
Fiber 6 g

Saucy Broccoli

Crisp, tender broccoli is the perfect side dish for any meal. Dress it up with your choice of savory sauces and it's ready for any occasion.

ingredient savvy

Broccolini

Sometimes called baby broccoli, broccolini is a cross between broccoli and Chinese kale, with long, thin stalks and a broccoli-like crown. Its flavor is a little sweeter than broccoli with a slightly peppery taste. Steam broccolini until crisp-tender and season it as you would broccoli.

Per serving with walnut sauce

Calories 89
Fat 8 g
Cholesterol 11 mg
Sodium 44 mg
Carbohydrate 4 g
Fiber 1 g

Per serving with almond sauce

Calories 78
Fat 6 g
Cholesterol 11 mg
Sodium 238 mg
Carbohydrate 5 g
Fiber 2 g

1 bunch (about 1 to 1¼ pounds) broccoli, trimmed
Lemon Walnut or Orange Almond Sauce (recipes follow)

Cut broccoli into spears. Place in microwave-safe dish; cover and microwave (high) for 5 minutes or until crisp-tender; drain. Place broccoli in serving dish. Drizzle sauce over top.

Makes 4-6 servings

Lemon Walnut Sauce

2 tablespoons butter
1 clove garlic, minced
1 teaspoon grated lemon peel
2 tablespoons fresh lemon juice
¼ cup chopped walnuts, toasted

Place butter and garlic in 2-cup glass measure. Microwave (high) for 45 seconds or until butter is melted. Stir in lemon peel and juice. Drizzle over cooked broccoli. Sprinkle walnuts over top.

Makes ½ cup

Orange Almond Sauce

2 tablespoons butter
2 teaspoons grated orange peel
2 tablespoons fresh orange juice
½ teaspoon salt
⅛ teaspoon ground white pepper
3 tablespoons sliced almonds, toasted

Place butter in 1-cup glass measure. Microwave (high) for 45 seconds or until melted. Stir in orange peel and juice, salt, and pepper. Drizzle over cooked broccoli. Sprinkle almonds over top.

Makes ½ cup

Glazed Carrots

Toss sweet, tender carrots with a tempting glaze for a sensational side dish. Each one is simple and delicious.

1 pound carrots, sliced diagonally
    1/4-inch thick

APRICOT GLAZE
1/4 cup apricot preserves
1 tablespoon butter or margarine
2 teaspoons fresh lemon juice

Place carrots in steamer basket. Place in covered saucepan with about 1 inch of water. Bring to a boil over high heat; reduce heat and steam until carrots are crisp-tender, about 10 minutes. Place all glaze ingredients in 1-cup glass measure. Microwave (high) for 30 to 45 seconds or until butter is melted; stir until well blended. Toss with cooked carrots. Garnish with lemon twist.

Makes 4-6 servings

Glaze Variations

DIJON GLAZE Omit preserves and lemon juice in glaze. Add 1 tablespoon brown sugar and 1 tablespoon dijon-style mustard to the 1 tablespoon butter.

Per serving with dijon glaze
Calories 57; Fat 2 g; Cholesterol 5 mg; Sodium 76 mg; Carbohydrate 9 g; Fiber 2 g

 Per serving with dijon glaze made with margarine
Calories 56; Fat 2 g; Cholesterol <1 mg; Sodium 81 mg; Carbohydrate 9 g; Fiber 2 g

HONEY LIME GLAZE Omit preserves and lemon juice in glaze. Add 1 tablespoon honey, 1 teaspoon grated lime peel, and 1 tablespoon fresh lime juice to the 1 tablespoon butter.

Per serving with honey lime glaze
Calories 57; Fat 2 g; Cholesterol 5 mg; Sodium 61 mg; Carbohydrate 10 g; Fiber 2 g

Per serving with honey lime glaze made with margarine
Calories 56; Fat 2 g; Cholesterol 0 mg; Sodium 66 mg; Carbohydrate 10 g; Fiber 2 g

technique savvy

Microwaving Vegetables

The microwave will quickly cook vegetables while retaining their flavor, color, and nutrients. Uniform-sized pieces cook evenly in a covered bowl with a few tablespoons of water. Stir halfway through the cooking time. Let them stand, covered, for one to two minutes to allow for carry-over cooking. Most vegetables cook in six minutes per pound on high (100% power).

Per serving with apricot glaze

Calories 78
Fat 2 g
Cholesterol 0 mg
Sodium 71 mg
Carbohydrate 15 g
Fiber 2 g

Grilled Corn-On-The-Cob

The season for fresh corn is short and sweet, so don't miss a single bite! Whether you cook it over the coals or in the microwave, slather on a flavorful butter for a special summer treat.

technique savvy

Microwaving Corn

The easiest way to cook corn-on-the-cob is in the microwave! Remove just the dark outer husk, leaving the remaining husk intact. Place up to six ears in the microwave, arranging in a spoke fashion. Microwave on high (100% power) for two minutes per ear and let the corn stand for several minutes. Pull back the husk, and the silk will come right off.

6 ears corn-on-the-cob in husk
Butter
Salt and pepper to taste

Remove tassles and large outer husks from corn. Soak corn in husks in cold water for 20 minutes. Place corn on grid over medium-high heat. Grill, turning frequently until kernels are bright yellow and tender, about 12 to 15 minutes. Remove husks and silk from corn. Serve with butter; season with salt and pepper.

Makes 6 servings

Flavored Butters

PARMESAN BUTTER In medium bowl with hand mixer, beat 1/2 cup softened butter, 1/4 cup grated parmesan cheese, 1/4 cup mayonnaise, and 1/2 teaspoon garlic powder until smooth.

Per ear of corn with I tablespoon parmesan butter
Calories 189; Fat 13 g; Cholesterol 25 mg; Sodium 123 mg; Carbohydrate 18 g; Fiber 2 g

SUN-DRIED TOMATO BUTTER In medium bowl with hand mixer, beat 1/2 cup softened butter, 1/4 cup sun-dried tomato spread, and 1/4 teaspoon garlic pepper until smooth.

Per ear of corn with I tablespoon tomato butter
Calories 157; Fat 10 g; Cholesterol 22 mg; Sodium 120 mg; Carbohydrate 18 g; Fiber 2 g

HERB BUTTER In medium bowl with hand mixer, beat 1/2 cup softened butter until light and fluffy. Stir in 1/3 cup finely chopped fresh basil and 1 teaspoon grated lemon peel until well blended.

Per ear of corn with I tablespoon herb butter
Calories 196; Fat 13 g; Cholesterol 32 mg; Sodium 100 mg; Carbohydrate 17 g; Fiber 3 g

TIP Flavored butters are also good on other vegetables, such as green beans, zucchini, asparagus, potatoes, or carrots; melted over pasta; or spread on warm bread.

Make-Ahead Mashed Potatoes

Rich, smooth, and creamy mashed potatoes without the last-minute fuss? You bet! No matter which of the tempting versions you prepare, it's the perfect dish to serve a crowd!

technique savvy

Freezing Mashed Potatoes

This make-ahead recipe is great for serving a crowd and even handier if you freeze it ahead. Prepare potatoes according to recipe directions but do not bake. Cover and freeze for up to one month. Thaw in refrigerator overnight and bake, covered, for 30 minutes. Uncover and bake about 15 minutes until heated through and lightly browned on top.

Per serving

Calories 166
Fat 4 g
Cholesterol 12 mg
Sodium 264 mg
Carbohydrate 26 g
Fiber 3 g

5 pounds russet potatoes, peeled, quartered, and cooked
1 large onion, finely chopped (optional)
1 package (8 ounces) light cream cheese, softened
1 cup milk
1 teaspoon salt
1 teaspoon ground black pepper
1 tablespoon chopped fresh parsley (optional)

In large bowl, mash together all ingredients except parsley until well blended and smooth. Spoon into lightly greased 9×13-inch baking dish that has been coated with no-stick cooking spray. Cover and refrigerate overnight. Bake covered in 350°F oven for 30 minutes. Uncover and bake until heated through and lightly browned on top, about 15 minutes. If desired, garnish with parsley.

Makes 10-12 servings

TIP If desired, potatoes may be mashed and served immediately without baking.

Variations

Add extra ingredients to potatoes before mashing:
ASIAGO MASHED POTATOES 2/3 cup grated asiago
ROASTED GARLIC MASHED POTATOES 2 to 4 cloves roasted garlic
HORSERADISH MASHED POTATOES 1 to 2 tablespoons prepared horseradish

White Cheddar Scalloped Potatoes

You won't believe something this good could be so easy! Yukon gold potatoes add a buttery, rich texture. Try them alongside baked ham, roast beef, or chicken.

3 pounds Yukon gold, butter, or
    russet potatoes, peeled and
    thinly sliced
Salt and ground white pepper
    to taste
8 ounces white cheddar cheese,
    shredded (about 2 cups)
1 cup heavy whipping cream

Arrange about one-third of the potato slices in greased 9×13-inch baking dish; season with salt and pepper. Top with one-third of the cheese. Repeat layering of potatoes, cheese, and seasoning to make 3 layers. Pour cream over potatoes. Cover and bake in 400°F oven for 45 minutes. Uncover and bake until golden brown, about 10 to 15 minutes.

Makes 10-12 servings

TIP It is not necessary to peel potatoes before slicing.

Cooking with Cream

When a recipe requires a long cooking time at a high temperature, it's best to use heavy whipping cream. It contains the fat necessary to prevent curdling. So, indulge and enjoy!

Per serving

Calories 209
Fat 14 g
Cholesterol 47 mg
Sodium 130 mg
Carbohydrate 15 g
Fiber 2 g

Sweet Potato Fries

These deliciously different crispy fries are a terrific side dish. Make plenty because they disappear quickly!

Deep-Fry Tips

Choose oils with a high smoke point for deep-fat frying, like peanut or vegetable oil. Don't use olive and specialty oils that break down at lower temperatures. Heat oil to 375°F. Drop a small piece of food into the fryer. If it pops up quickly, the oil is hot enough. Fry foods in small batches to maintain the oil temperature. Overcrowding the fryer lowers the temperature, causing food to taste greasy.

1 1/2 pounds sweet potatoes (about 2 to 3 potatoes)
1 cup (1/2 of 8-ounce package) tempura batter mix
1 teaspoon Old Bay seasoning
3/4 cup ice water
Vegetable oil for frying
Salt to taste

Peel potatoes; cut into 1/4-inch thick strips. In medium bowl, whisk together batter mix, seasoning, and ice water until smooth. In deep skillet or deep-fat fryer, heat 2 inches of oil to 375°F. Dip a few potato strips at a time into batter; shake off excess. Add strips, one at a time, to hot oil; do not crowd fryer. Cook, turning once, until evenly browned, about 3 to 5 minutes. Drain on paper towels. Sprinkle with salt or additional Old Bay seasoning to taste.

Makes 6 servings

TIP Remaining tempura batter mix can be wrapped in airtight bag or container and frozen for another use.

Per serving

Calories 451
Fat 37 g
Cholesterol 0 mg
Sodium 260 mg
Carbohydrate 30 g
Fiber 3 g

Gratin of Summer Squash

This absolutely wonderful dish can be a meal in itself. Layers of tender herbed vegetables and creamy fontina cheese bake to bubbly perfection beneath a crispy crumb topping.

contributed by

Jennifer Kassel

Staff Home Economist Jennifer Kassel has been the manager of the Southroads School of Cooking since 1998. Always "into" food, she describes herself as the "kid who would try anything." Jennifer's creative classes span the culinary spectrum from tempting appetizers to wine country classics, with the occasional nod to all things lemon. Rich cheeses and fragrant herbs are her favorite ingredients, so it's no surprise that they are the inspiration for some of her most popular recipes.

1 tablespoon butter
1 large onion, thinly sliced
3 tablespoons fresh thyme (divided)
2 medium tomatoes
2 small yellow squash
1 medium zucchini
2 to 3 tablespoons olive oil
1/2 teaspoon coarse salt
8 ounces fontina cheese, shredded (about 2 cups)
1/4 cup dry bread crumbs

In medium skillet, melt butter over medium heat. Add onion and half of the thyme; toss to mix evenly. Cook until onions are caramelized, about 10 minutes. Meanwhile, slice tomatoes; place on plate to drain. Thinly slice squash and zucchini; toss with olive oil, salt, and remaining thyme. Place caramelized onions in 2-quart shallow baking dish that has been coated with no-stick cooking spray. Layer half of the squash and zucchini slices over onion; top with half of the tomatoes and half of the cheese. Repeat layers. Sprinkle bread crumbs over top. Bake in 375°F oven until top is browned, about 50 to 60 minutes.

Makes 6-8 servings

Per serving

Calories 205
Fat 15 g
Cholesterol 42 mg
Sodium 419 mg
Carbohydrate 8 g
Fiber 2 g

Oven-Roasted Cauliflower

Roasting vegetables brings out their natural sweetness and makes an ordinary side dish something special. Just a drizzle of olive oil and your favorite seasonings are all you need.

1 medium head cauliflower, cut into bite-sized pieces
1 tablespoon olive oil
1 teaspoon lemon herb seasoning
Coarse salt to taste
Diced pimiento, well drained (optional)

Place cauliflower pieces on lightly greased 10×15-inch jellyroll pan. Drizzle with olive oil; sprinkle with lemon seasoning. Toss well to coat. Spread cauliflower in single layer. Roast in 400°F oven, stirring halfway through cooking time, until cauliflower is tender and golden brown, about 25 minutes. Season with salt. If desired, sprinkle pimiento over top.

Makes 6-8 servings

TIP If desired, substitute Old Bay seasoning or lemon pepper seasoning for lemon herb seasoning.

Roasting Vegetables

Roasting vegetables caramelizes their sugars and brings out their natural sweetness. Cut vegetables of similar texture into same-size pieces and place on a lightly greased jellyroll pan. Drizzle lightly with olive oil, tossing to coat. Sprinkle with salt, pepper, and herbs, if desired. Roast in a 400°F oven for 20 to 30 minutes, stirring halfway through cooking time, until tender.

Per serving cauliflower

Calories 25
Fat 2 g
Cholesterol 0 mg
Sodium 86 mg
Carbohydrate 2 g
Fiber 1 g

Per serving green beans

Calories 68
Fat 4 g
Cholesterol 11 mg
Sodium 35 mg
Carbohydrate 7 g
Fiber 4 g

Green Beans with Gremolata

Gremolata, an Italian garnish of grated lemon peel, garlic, and parsley, adds a bright, lively flavor to fresh green beans.

1½ pounds green beans, trimmed
2 tablespoons butter or margarine, melted
1 tablespoon minced fresh Italian parsley
1½ teaspoons grated lemon peel
1 clove garlic, minced
Salt and pepper to taste

In large saucepan of boiling water, cook green beans until crisp-tender, about 7 minutes; drain. Place beans in serving bowl. Drizzle melted butter over beans. In small bowl, stir together parsley, lemon peel, and garlic. Sprinkle over beans; toss until well mixed. Season with salt and pepper.

Makes 6 servings

Microwave Hollandaise Sauce

This no-fail hollandaise sauce is rich, smooth, and delicious—every time! It's the perfect finishing touch for steamed broccoli or asparagus, baked fish, or your favorite egg dishes.

1/2 cup butter

3 egg yolks, slightly beaten

2 tablespoons heavy whipping
cream

2 tablespoons fresh lemon juice

1/2 teaspoon dry mustard

1/4 teaspoon salt

2 to 3 drops hot pepper sauce

Place butter in 2-cup glass measure. Microwave (high) for 1 minute or until melted; set aside. In small bowl, combine egg yolks, cream, lemon juice, dry mustard, salt, and hot sauce. Whisk until smooth. Slowly whisk egg mixture into melted butter. Microwave (medium-50% power) for 1 minute, whisking every 20 seconds, until sauce is thick and smooth.

Makes 1 cup

Per 2 tablespoons

Calories 143

Fat 15 g

Cholesterol 114 mg

Sodium 165 mg

Carbohydrate 1 g

Fiber 0 g

Lemon Aïoli

Spiked with lemon, capers, and garlic, this simple sauce will turn crab cakes and grilled fish into something special. Try it as a dip with fresh vegetables, too.

1/2 cup mayonnaise

1/2 cup dairy sour cream

2 tablespoons capers, rinsed
and drained

1 tablespoon minced fresh
Italian parsley

1 clove garlic, minced

2 teaspoons dijon-style mustard

1 teaspoon grated lemon peel

In small bowl, combine all ingredients; stir to blend. Place in covered container and refrigerate for up to 3 days.

Makes 1 cup

Per 2 tablespoons

Calories 128

Fat 13 g

Cholesterol 11 mg

Sodium 140 mg

Carbohydrate 2 g

Fiber <1 g

entrées and more

From the Grill

Raspberry Balsamic Marinade

Per $^1/_2$ cup

Calories 559
Fat 27 g
Cholesterol 0 mg
Sodium 39 mg
Carbohydrate 75 g
Fiber 1 g

1/4 cup balsamic vinegar
1/4 cup seedless raspberry jam
2 tablespoons olive oil
1 clove garlic, minced
1/2 teaspoon dried thyme, crushed
1/4 teaspoon ground black pepper

In small bowl, stir together all ingredients. Use to marinate chicken or pork.

Makes 1/2 cup

Caribbean Glaze

Per 2 tablespoons

Calories 83
Fat <1 g
Cholesterol 0 mg
Sodium 116 mg
Carbohydrate 17 g
Fiber 1 g

1 jar (9 ounces) chopped chutney
1/2 cup firmly packed brown sugar
1/4 cup stone ground mustard
1/4 cup dark rum

In work bowl of food processor fitted with steel knife blade or in blender container, combine all ingredients. Process until smooth. In small saucepan, heat sauce mixture over medium-high heat until boiling. Remove from heat; reserve about half to serve as sauce. Spoon remaining glaze over ribs, pork, or chicken during last 10 minutes of grilling.

Makes 1 1/2 cups

Spicy Rub

Per 1 tablespoon

Calories 40
Fat 1 g
Cholesterol 0 mg
Sodium 34 mg
Carbohydrate 9 g
Fiber 1 g

1/4 cup firmly packed brown sugar
3 tablespoons chili powder
2 teaspoons ground coriander
2 teaspoons ground cumin
1 1/2 teaspoons garlic powder
1 teaspoon dried oregano
1/2 teaspoon ground cayenne pepper

In small bowl, combine all ingredients; spread mixture on sheet of waxed paper. Before grilling, press mixture into beef steaks, pork chops, or pork roast until all surfaces are coated.

Makes 1/2 cup

Tomato Avocado Bruschetta

Start a special patio dinner with a simple yet sophisticated appetizer. Just grill slices of crusty bread, then top them with creamy cheese spread and fresh summer vegetables.

3 tablespoons extra virgin olive oil

2 tablespoons white balsamic or
    white wine vinegar

1/2 teaspoon salt

1 box (10 ounces) grape tomatoes,
    quartered, or 11/2 cups chopped
    tomatoes, well drained

1 avocado, seeded, peeled,
    and diced

1 to 2 cloves garlic, minced

2 tablespoons slivered fresh basil

1 package (4 ounces) goat cheese,
    softened

1 package (3 ounces) cream
    cheese, softened

1 loaf (16 ounces) sliced Italian bread

Olive oil for grilling bread

In medium bowl, combine olive oil, vinegar, and salt; whisk until well blended. Add tomatoes, avocado, garlic, and basil; toss gently. In small bowl, combine cheeses until evenly blended; chill until ready to assemble. Brush 12 slices of bread with olive oil; place on grid over medium heat. (Reserve remaining bread for other uses.) Grill until toasted on both sides. Spread cheese mixture over toast. Cut each slice in half. Top with tomato mixture.

Makes 2 dozen appetizers

c u i s i n e   s a v v y

What Is Bruschetta?

Bruschetta are tasty little toasts that are terrific for entertaining! Grill or toast the bread up to 24 hours ahead of time, if desired, and store loosely covered at room temperature. When guests arrive, add the flavorful toppings and enjoy!

Per 2 appetizers

Calories 167

Fat 11 g

Cholesterol 12 mg

Sodium 261 mg

Carbohydrate 14 g

Fiber 2 g

Lemon Grilled Asparagus

The flavor of grilled asparagus is simply sublime. So simple, so delicious—it may become your favorite way to cook asparagus!

technique savvy

Juicing Citrus Fruit

When limes, lemons, or oranges are still hard, place in the microwave for 30 seconds before juicing. Membranes will loosen, giving you the most juice from the fruit. An average lime yields about two tablespoons of juice, a lemon yields about one-fourth cup juice, and an orange about one-half cup juice.

1 pound asparagus, trimmed
2 tablespoons olive oil
1 large clove garlic, minced
1 teaspoon grated lemon peel
Coarse salt and coarsely ground
    black pepper to taste

Place asparagus on platter. In small bowl, combine olive oil, garlic, and lemon peel. Drizzle over asparagus; toss to coat. Season with salt and pepper. Place diagonally on grid over medium-high heat; grill until crisp-tender and slightly charred, about 5 to 7 minutes.

Makes 4 servings

Per serving

Calories 74
Fat 7 g
Cholesterol 0 mg
Sodium 2 mg
Carbohydrate 3 g
Fiber 1 g

Garlic Grilled Potato Salad

Potatoes cooked over the coals are golden brown and delicious. You'll find yourself making this simple side dish again and again.

ingredient savvy

Russets or Reds?

Potato varieties are different in texture, so be sure to choose the right one for the job. Russet potatoes are low in moisture and high in starch, which give French fries, baked, and mashed potatoes their light, fluffy texture. Red potatoes are higher in moisture and lower in starch, so they hold their shape well after cooking. They're ideal for soups, salads, and casseroles. Either variety cooks well on the grill.

2 shallots, coarsely chopped
4 cloves garlic, coarsely chopped
2 tablespoons olive oil (divided)
2 pounds red potatoes, quartered
  lengthwise
1/2 cup dairy sour cream
1/2 cup mayonnaise
1/4 cup chopped fresh parsley
2 tablespoons red wine vinegar
Salt and pepper to taste

Combine shallots and garlic on sheet of heavy-duty foil. Drizzle with 1 teaspoon of the olive oil. Fold foil into tightly sealed packet. In large bowl, toss potatoes with remaining olive oil until coated. Place potatoes on grid over medium heat; grill, turning occasionally until tender, about 20 minutes. Place foil packet on grid; grill, turning occasionally until packet puffs slightly and shallots and garlic are golden, about 12 minutes. In medium bowl, combine roasted shallots and garlic with remaining ingredients. Cut warm potatoes into bite-sized pieces; toss with dressing. Best served warm or at room temperature.

Makes 6 servings

Per serving

Calories 323
Fat 23 g
Cholesterol 14 mg
Sodium 120 mg
Carbohydrate 26 g
Fiber 3 g

Summer Vegetable Medley

Grilling brings out the natural sweetness of bountiful summer vegetables. Toss them with freshly cooked pasta and select seasonings for a deliciously light warm-weather meal.

1 small eggplant, cut crosswise into
   1/2-inch thick slices
2 large bell peppers (red, yellow or
   orange), quartered and seeded
1 medium zucchini,
   quartered lengthwise
1 medium yellow squash,
   quartered lengthwise
Extra virgin olive oil
Coarse salt and ground black pepper
   to taste

Place vegetables on tray. Brush all sides of vegetables lightly with olive oil. Sprinkle with salt and pepper. Place vegetables on grid over medium-high heat; grill, turning frequently and brushing with oil as needed until tender and lightly charred, about 8 to 10 minutes for eggplant; about 6 to 8 minutes for peppers and squash. Season with salt and pepper.

Makes 4-6 servings

ingredient savvy

Orzo Pasta

Orzo and rosamarina are tiny-grained pastas that look a lot like rice. They are most often used in soups, but are also terrific used in place of rice in all sorts of dishes. Cook orzo and rosamarina al dente, or just until tender, like other pastas. Then use them as a base for pasta salads or as a bed for your favorite grilled kabobs.

Greek Orzo Salad

Cook 1 1/2 cups orzo pasta (rosamarina) according to package directions. Cut grilled vegetables into bite-sized pieces. Stir into pasta along with 1 can (2 1/4 ounces) sliced ripe olives, drained; grated peel and juice of 1 small lemon; 2 ounces (1/2 cup) crumbled feta cheese; and 2 tablespoons extra virgin olive oil. Serve immediately, or cover and chill for several hours. Makes 6-8 servings

 Per entrée serving
   Calories 213; Fat 7 g; Cholesterol 5 mg; Sodium 172 mg; Carbohydrate 33 g; Fiber 5 g

Summer Penne Pasta

Cook 8 ounces penne pasta according to package directions. Cut grilled vegetables into bite-sized pieces. Stir into pasta along with juice of 1/2 lemon; 1/4 cup chopped fresh Italian parsley; and 2 tablespoons extra virgin olive oil. Grate parmesan cheese over top. Serve immediately, or cover and chill for several hours. Makes 6-8 servings

 Per entrée serving
   Calories 170; Fat 4 g; Cholesterol 0 mg; Sodium 8 mg; Carbohydrate 29 g; Fiber 4 g

**Per serving
vegetable medley**

Calories 44
Fat <1 g
Cholesterol 0 mg
Sodium 7 mg
Carbohydrate 10 g
Fiber 5 g

Java Steak with Glazed Shiitake Mushrooms

A coffee liqueur marinade gives this steak a deep, rich flavor. It also makes a delicious glaze for the sautéed mushrooms served alongside.

1¹/2 to 2 pounds beef sirloin or
    London broil (top round), about
    1 inch thick
¹/2 cup soy sauce
¹/2 cup coffee-flavored liqueur
    (Kahlúa, Tía Maria)
1 tablespoon cracked black pepper
1 tablespoon butter
1 tablespoon vegetable oil
¹/2 pound shiitake mushrooms,
    stemmed and caps sliced
Salt and pepper to taste

Place steak in large freezer-weight reclosable plastic bag. In small bowl, stir together soy sauce and liqueur. Pour half of the mixture over steak; reserve remaining mixture for mushrooms. Seal bag and turn to coat meat. Place bag on plate and marinate in refrigerator for 2 to 4 hours for sirloin, or overnight for London broil. Remove steak from bag; discard marinade. Pat steak dry with paper towels. Spread cracked pepper on sheet of waxed paper. Roll steak in pepper until lightly coated. Let steak stand at room temperature for about 15 minutes. In large skillet, heat butter and oil over medium-high heat. Add shiitakes; cover and cook until tender, about 3 minutes. Stir in reserved soy sauce mixture. Cook uncovered until most of liquid evaporates and mushrooms are glazed, about 5 minutes. Season with salt and pepper. Remove from heat; let stand while grilling steak.

Place steak on grid over medium-high heat; grill until internal temperature is 145°F for medium-rare, about 4 to 5 minutes per side. Remove from grill and let stand for 5 minutes before thinly slicing across the grain. Serve with glazed mushrooms.

Makes 6-8 servings

contributed by

Therese Lewis

Staff Home Economist and former School of Cooking Manager, Therese Lewis has been teaching cooking classes since 1981. Her grandmother taught her how to make pierogies when she was in grade school and cooking has been her passion ever since. Therese writes copy for *Everybody Cooks®* magazine, Dierbergs.com, and Dierbergs Presents *Everybody Cooks®* television show. Hot, spicy dishes are her signature, but combining familiar ingredients in unexpected ways is what gives her recipes a delicious element of surprise.

Per 3-ounce cooked portion with margarine

Calories 273
Fat 9 g
Cholesterol 76 mg
Sodium 549 mg
Carbohydrate 4 g
Fiber <1 g

Steak with Blue Cheese Butter

A flavorful red wine marinade tenderizes London broil. A pat of blue cheese butter is a savory finishing touch.

Steak Secrets

Let steak stand at room temperature for fifteen minutes before grilling.

Sprinkle on salt just before cooking.

For perfect grill marks, sear steaks over direct high heat.

Allow steak to rest for three to five minutes before slicing.

1 1/2 pounds London broil, about 1 inch thick
1/2 cup dry red wine
3 tablespoons olive oil
2 tablespoons Worcestershire sauce
2 cloves garlic, minced
1/2 teaspoon seasoned salt
1/4 cup butter, softened
1/4 cup blue cheese crumbles
1 tablespoon snipped fresh chives

Place meat in large freezer-weight reclosable plastic bag. In 1-cup glass measure, combine wine, olive oil, Worcestershire, garlic, and seasoned salt. Pour over meat; seal bag and turn to coat meat. Place bag on plate and marinate in refrigerator for 4 to 24 hours. In small bowl, blend butter, blue cheese, and chives. Remove steak from bag; discard marinade. Place steak on grid over medium-high heat; grill until internal temperature is 145°F for medium-rare, about 5 to 8 minutes per side. Remove from grill; let stand for 5 minutes before thinly slicing across the grain. Serve with blue cheese butter.

Makes 6 servings

TIP London broil is known as top round steak in some areas.

Per serving

Calories 297
Fat 20 g
Cholesterol 74 mg
Sodium 263 mg
Carbohydrate <1 g
Fiber 0 g

Pepper-Jack Burgers

Great restaurant-style burgers are right in your own backyard! Topped with melting pepper-jack cheese, grilled peppers and onions, and a zesty sauce, these are sure to be a hit.

1/4 cup mayonnaise
2 tablespoons salsa
1 clove garlic, minced
1 red bell pepper, quartered
1 medium onion, sliced
Olive oil
1 1/2 pounds lean ground beef
6 slices pepper-jack cheese
6 hamburger buns

In small bowl, stir together mayonnaise, salsa, and garlic; chill. Place bell pepper and onion slices on sheet of foil; brush with olive oil. Place foil on grid over medium-high heat; grill, turning occasionally until softened and lightly browned, about 10 to 12 minutes. Cut pepper into strips; separate onion into rings. Divide beef into 6 portions and shape into patties. Place on grid over medium-high heat; grill until internal temperature is 160°F, about 5 to 6 minutes per side. Top burgers with cheese; grill until melted. Toast cut sides of buns on grill. Top with burgers and vegetables. Serve with salsa mayonnaise.

Makes 6 servings

Selecting Ground Beef

When selecting ground beef for a recipe, choose a grind with enough fat to deliver just the right amount of moisture and flavor! For chili or spaghetti, very lean beef with a fat content of as little as 4 percent fat will do the trick. For patties and meatloaf, a little higher fat content (15-20%) will provide moisture, hold its shape without crumbling, and ensure a juicy entrée that's easy to slice.

Per serving

Calories 553
Fat 35 g
Cholesterol 109 mg
Sodium 517 mg
Carbohydrate 26 g
Fiber 2 g

Baby Burgers with Caramelized Onions

These miniature burgers make any barbecue more fun and leave room to sample everything else on the menu. Smothered in sweet caramelized onions and stuffed with creamy cheese, they're a special treat!

Caramelizing Onions

Slow, even cooking allows the natural sugars present in food to caramelize, adding a rich, mellow sweetness and deep golden brown color.

Onions will caramelize more evenly when cooked in an untreated skillet rather than one with a nonstick coating. Cook them slowly over low heat so they don't burn. Sprinkle with a pinch of sugar to speed up the process and add a little extra sweetness.

1 pound lean ground beef
1/2 pound ground pork
1 egg, slightly beaten
1/2 teaspoon salt
1/4 teaspoon cracked black pepper
8 ounces fontina, gouda, or blue cheese, cut into twelve 1/2-inch cubes
24 thin slices French baguette, toasted
Caramelized Onions (recipe follows)

In medium bowl, combine ground beef, pork, egg, salt, and pepper; mix gently. Divide evenly into 24 portions and shape into thin patties. Place 1 cube of cheese on 12 of the patties. Cover with remaining patties; press edges with tines of fork to seal. Place on grid over medium heat; grill until well done and no longer pink, about 4 minutes per side. Serve on toasted baguette slices topped with Caramelized Onions.

Makes 12 baby burgers

Caramelized Onions

1 tablespoon butter
1 jumbo onion, thinly sliced
1 teaspoon sugar
1/2 teaspoon coarse salt
1/4 teaspoon cracked black pepper
2 tablespoons water

In medium skillet, melt butter over medium-high heat. Add onion, sugar, salt, and pepper. Cook, stirring frequently until onion is browned and caramelized, about 15 minutes. Stir in water, scraping browned bits from bottom of pan. Cook until onions are tender and water evaporates.

Makes about 1 1/2 cups

TIP Onions may be caramelized ahead and refrigerated. Reheat before serving.

Per baby burger with 1 tablespoon onions

Calories 219
Fat 12 g
Cholesterol 81 mg
Sodium 429 mg
Carbohydrate 8 g
Fiber <1 g

Grilled Pork Tenderloin with Mango Salsa

contributed by

Linda Behrends

Home Economist Linda Behrends launched the first Dierbergs School of Cooking in 1978, and two additional schools soon thereafter. Her passion for cooking and commitment to introducing people to good food easily prepared at home set the stage for a future of exciting classes and delicious recipes. Linda is a food marketing consultant and talented food stylist. Her creativity has graced the photos in Dierbergs *Everybody Cooks®* magazine since 1985.

2 pork tenderloins
    (about 1¼ pounds each)
¼ cup firmly packed brown sugar
¼ cup fresh lime juice
¼ cup vegetable oil
2 cloves garlic, crushed
1 tablespoon chili powder
1 teaspoon ground coriander
1 teaspoon ground cumin
¼ teaspoon crushed red pepper
    flakes, or ⅛ teaspoon ground
    cayenne pepper

Trim fat and silver skin from tenderloins. Place pork in large freezer-weight reclosable plastic bag. In small bowl, stir together remaining ingredients. Pour over meat; seal bag and turn to coat pork. Place bag on plate and marinate in refrigerator for 2 to 4 hours. Remove pork from bag; discard marinade. Pat dry with paper towels. Place tenderloins on grid over medium heat; grill, turning occasionally until internal temperature is 155°F, about 25 to 35 minutes. (Pork is done when there is still a hint of pink in center.) Let rest for 10 minutes before slicing diagonally ½-inch thick. Serve with Mango Salsa.

Makes 8 servings

Mango Salsa

2 ripe mangoes
¼ red bell pepper, finely chopped
¼ medium red onion, finely diced
1 jalapeño pepper, seeded and finely
    chopped (optional)
2 tablespoons chopped fresh cilantro
¼ teaspoon grated lime peel
2 tablespoons fresh lime juice
1 tablespoon olive oil
1 clove garlic, minced
¼ teaspoon Cajun/Creole seasoning
Salt and coarsely ground black
    pepper to taste

With sharp knife, cut flesh of mango from seed. Remove peel and dice. In medium bowl, combine mangoes, bell pepper, onion, jalapeño, and cilantro. In small bowl, combine remaining ingredients. Pour over mango mixture; toss gently to coat.

Makes 2 cups

Per 3-ounce cooked portion with ¼ cup salsa

Calories 172
Fat 5 g
Cholesterol 84 mg
Sodium 61 mg
Carbohydrate 2 g
Fiber <1 g

Southwest Tostada Salad

The sunny flavors of the Southwest come together in this satisfying main-dish salad. It's fabulous with chicken or beef!

Instant-Read Thermometers

The best way to determine doneness of meat is by checking the internal temperature. Insert an instant-read thermometer into the thickest portion of the meat, being sure that it doesn't touch the bone or a pocket of fat. When testing thin cuts like chicken breasts, steaks, or burgers, insert the thermometer horizontally into the meat.

Per serving with chicken

Calories 581
Fat 28 g
Cholesterol 84 mg
Sodium 918 mg
Carbohydrate 46 g
Fiber 8 g

Per serving with beef

Calories 663
Fat 35 g
Cholesterol 107 mg
Sodium 929 mg
Carbohydrate 46 g
Fiber 8 g

5 tablespoons vegetable oil (divided)
1 teaspoon ground cumin (divided)
1/2 teaspoon chili powder
6 large flour tortillas (8-inch diameter)
1/3 cup red wine vinegar
3/4 cup salsa
1/4 teaspoon salt
1 pound boneless, skinless chicken breast halves
1 can (15 ounces) black beans, rinsed and drained
1 can (7 ounces) corn, drained
1/2 cup coarsely chopped red onion
1 large tomato, chopped
Shredded lettuce
8 ounces hot pepper cheese, shredded (about 2 cups)

In small bowl, combine 2 tablespoons of the oil with 1/2 teaspoon of the cumin and the chili powder. Brush on both sides of each flour tortilla. Place directly on grid over medium-high heat; grill until golden brown and crisp, about 1 to 2 minutes per side. If tortillas bubble up, pierce surface to flatten. Remove tortillas from heat; cool completely.

In medium bowl, whisk together remaining 3 tablespoons oil and vinegar. Stir in salsa, remaining 1/2 teaspoon cumin, and salt. Remove 1/2 cup of the salsa mixture for basting chicken; reserve remaining salsa mixture for dressing. Place chicken on grid over medium-high heat; grill, basting occasionally with salsa mixture, until internal temperature is 165°F, about 5 to 6 minutes per side. Cut chicken into strips. In medium bowl, toss together beans, corn, onion, tomato, and reserved dressing. To assemble, place grilled tortilla on plate. Top with shredded lettuce and 1 cup of the vegetable mixture. Top with chicken strips and shredded cheese.

Makes 6 servings

Southwest Beef Tostada Salad

Substitute 1 pound sirloin steak for chicken. Trim fat from meat. Place meat in large freezer-weight reclosable plastic bag. Reserve 3/4 cup of salsa mixture for dressing; add remaining salsa mixture to meat. Seal bag; turn to coat meat. Place bag on plate; marinate in refrigerator at least 30 minutes or up to 24 hours. Remove meat from bag; discard marinade. Place meat on grid over medium-high heat; grill until internal temperature is 145°F for medium-rare, about 5 to 6 minutes per side. Cut into thin strips. Assemble as directed.

Grilled Adobo Chicken

This tangy citrus marinade gets a touch of smoky heat from puréed chipotle chiles. Try it on steak or pork tenderloin, too.

6 boneless, skinless chicken breast halves (about 1½ pounds)

½ cup frozen orange juice concentrate, thawed

2 tablespoons puréed chipotle chiles in adobo sauce

1 tablespoon vegetable oil

1 teaspoon dried basil

¼ teaspoon salt

¼ teaspoon ground cinnamon

Place chicken in large freezer-weight reclosable plastic bag. In small bowl, stir together remaining ingredients. Pour over chicken; seal bag and turn to coat chicken. Place bag on plate and marinate in refrigerator for up to 8 hours. Remove chicken from bag; discard marinade. Place chicken on grid over medium-high heat; grill until internal temperature is 165°F, about 6 minutes per side.

Makes 6 servings

ingredient savvy

Chipotles in Adobo Sauce

Chipotles (chih-POHT-lays)— those little hot peppers with wrinkled, dark red skin—are actually smoked jalapeños. They are generally canned in adobo sauce, a piquant blend of tomatoes and spices. Because just a little bit of pepper adds a big burst of flavor, purée the chiles with the sauce and freeze the purée in a freezer-weight plastic bag. Break off a piece as needed to add a touch of smoky heat to mayonnaise, dips, chili—all sorts of dishes.

Per serving

Calories 92

Fat 1 g

Cholesterol 43 mg

Sodium 60 mg

Carbohydrate 2 g

Fiber <1 g

Spicy Thai Chicken Pasta

A bold and spicy marinade gives these grilled chicken skewers lively Asian flavor. Serve them on a bed of pasta tossed with crisp stir-fried vegetables for a complete meal.

technique savvy

Safe Marinating

For food safety, always marinate in the refrigerator, whether marinating meat for 30 minutes or overnight. Place meat in a reclosable plastic bag or non-metal container to avoid a metallic flavor. Always discard marinade that has come in contact with raw meat. If you plan to serve the marinade as a sauce, double the marinade and set half of it aside.

4 boneless, skinless chicken breast halves (about 1 pound)
1 cup chicken broth
1/3 cup creamy peanut butter
1/3 cup soy sauce
2 tablespoons brown sugar
2 tablespoons fresh lemon juice
1 teaspoon minced fresh ginger root
1 teaspoon minced garlic
1/2 teaspoon crushed red pepper flakes
1 package (16 ounces) linguine
1 package (16 ounces) fresh vegetable stir-fry medley

Place chicken breasts between sheets of plastic wrap; lightly pound to even thickness. Cut into 1-inch strips. Place in large freezer-weight reclosable plastic bag. In 4-cup glass measure, combine chicken broth, peanut butter, soy sauce, brown sugar, lemon juice, ginger, garlic, and red pepper flakes. Microwave (high) for 2 minutes or until peanut butter melts enough to mix smoothly. Place 1/2 cup of the marinade in bag with chicken; reserve remaining marinade. Seal bag; turn to coat chicken. Place bag on plate and marinate in refrigerator for 2 to 4 hours.

Remove chicken from bag and discard marinade. Weave chicken onto skewers. Place on oiled grid over medium-high heat; grill until no longer pink, about 4 to 5 minutes per side. Meanwhile, cook linguine in large pot of boiling water for 5 minutes; drain water. Add reserved marinade and vegetables. Cook until pasta is al dente and vegetables are tender, about 5 to 7 minutes. Place pasta on large platter. Top with skewers of grilled chicken.

Makes 6 servings

TIP If necessary, cut large pieces of vegetables into bite-size pieces to ensure even cooking.

Per serving

Calories 440
Fat 6 g
Cholesterol 44 mg
Sodium 527 mg
Carbohydrate 65 g
Fiber 4 g

Grilled Coconut Shrimp

Tender shrimp wrapped in a sweet and crispy coconut crust will win rave reviews at your next backyard gathering.

1½ pounds extra large or jumbo
    shrimp, peeled and deveined
⅓ cup flour
1 egg, beaten with 2 tablespoons
    water, OR ⅓ cup egg substitute
1 cup flaked coconut
½ cup dry bread crumbs
¼ teaspoon salt

Pat shrimp dry with paper towels. Place flour on sheet of waxed paper. Place egg mixture in shallow dish. In second shallow dish, combine coconut, bread crumbs, and salt. Coat shrimp with flour, dip into egg, then coat with coconut mixture. Thread shrimp onto skewers. Place on oiled grid over medium heat; grill until coating is toasted and shrimp are opaque, about 4 minutes per side. If desired, serve with Mango Salsa (recipe on page 122).

Makes 6 servings

TIP Shrimp may be broiled for 4 to 5 minutes per side.

Breading Hint

When a recipe calls for breading, think of egg substitute! Dip food in egg substitute instead of beaten egg before rolling in crumbs. It coats food more evenly, allowing crumbs to cover food completely.

Per serving

Calories 287
Fat 10 g
Cholesterol 208 mg
Sodium 407 mg
Carbohydrate 21 g
Fiber 2 g

Jammin' Jamaican Salmon

Rub salmon with a blend of brown sugar and zesty spices for a taste of the islands. Add Sweet Potato Fries (recipe on page 102) or grilled summer squash on the side.

technique savvy

Covering the Grill

To capture the great smoky flavor that grilling is all about, keep the cover on when cooking over the coals. This allows the heat to circulate evenly and prevents flare-ups.

1½ pounds salmon fillets
1 tablespoon brown sugar
1 teaspoon Old Bay seasoning
1 teaspoon Cajun/Creole seasoning
½ teaspoon ground nutmeg
Olive oil

Cut salmon into serving-sized pieces. In small bowl, combine remaining ingredients except oil. Brush flesh side of salmon with olive oil; rub with seasoning mixture. Place salmon, flesh-side down, on oiled grid over medium-high heat; cover and grill for 4 minutes. Turn fish skin-side down with large metal spatula. Grill until just opaque throughout, about 4 to 6 minutes.

Makes 6 servings

TIP For easy cleanup and serving, place sheet of heavy-duty foil on grid alongside salmon while it cooks flesh-side down. Turn fish and place skin-side down on top of preheated foil. When salmon is done, slide metal spatula between flesh and skin. (Skin will stick to foil.) Remove foil from grill and discard.

Lemon Rosemary Salmon

If desired, replace Jamaican seasonings (Old Bay, Cajun/Creole, and nutmeg) with 1 tablespoon snipped fresh rosemary, 2 teaspoons grated lemon peel, ½ teaspoon coarse salt, and ½ teaspoon coarsely ground black pepper.

Per 3-ounce cooked portion

Calories 190
Fat 9 g
Cholesterol 57 mg
Sodium 358 mg
Carbohydrate 2 g
Fiber 0 g

128

Lime Grilled Fish Steaks

A simple marinade with a splash of lime juice gives hearty tuna steaks a bright, fresh flavor.

1½ pounds tuna or swordfish steaks
Coarse salt and coarsely ground
    black pepper to taste
1 tablespoon brown sugar
1 teaspoon grated lime peel
1 tablespoon fresh lime juice
1 tablespoon vegetable oil

Season both sides of fish with salt and pepper. In small bowl, stir together remaining ingredients. Place fish on oiled grid over high heat; grill brushing generously with lime mixture until fish is opaque throughout, about 5 minutes per side. Do not overcook.

Makes 6 servings

TIP Measure the thickest part of the fish. As a guide, allow 10 minutes cooking time per inch of thickness.

technique savvy

Grilling Tuna

Fresh tuna has a rich, meaty texture and is cooked to perfection when the flesh turns opaque but is still slightly pink in the center. Like any cut of meat, tuna is very dry when it is overcooked. For best results, cook fresh tuna to an internal temperature of 145°F.

Per 3-ounce cooked portion

Calories 151
Fat 3 g
Cholesterol 51 mg
Sodium 43 mg
Carbohydrate 3 g
Fiber 0 g

Pesto Pizza on the Grill

You'll love the wonderful smoky flavor and crisp crust of pizza cooked on the grill. Garlicky pesto and colorful vegetables give it classic Mediterranean flavor.

Pizza Dough

Fast rising dry yeast is ideal for making homemade pizza crust. It does not need to be dissolved in liquid and needs only one rising, so your fresh, homemade pizza can be ready in less than an hour. Pizza dough can be made, tightly wrapped, and refrigerated for up to 48 hours. Before using, allow dough to stand at room temperature for 30 minutes. Then shape, add your favorite toppings, and bake!

2 cloves garlic, minced
1 tablespoon olive oil
1 small yellow squash, thinly sliced
1/2 cup sliced red onion
Super Simple Pizza Dough
    (recipe follows)
1/4 cup prepared pesto sauce
2 Roma tomatoes, thinly sliced
1 can (14 ounces) artichoke hearts
    in water, drained and quartered
1/3 cup shredded parmesan cheese
Thinly sliced fresh basil

In large skillet, cook garlic in olive oil over medium-high heat for 1 minute. Add squash and onion; cook until tender, about 5 to 6 minutes. Prepare pizza crust dough. Shape into rough 12-inch circle and place on floured pizza pan. Slide crust onto oiled grid over medium-high heat; grill until lightly browned on bottom, about 3 to 4 minutes. Turn crust over onto wooden board. Spread pesto sauce evenly over crust. Top with squash mixture. Arrange tomatoes and artichokes over top. Slide onto grid; cover and grill until crust is lightly browned on bottom, about 3 to 4 minutes. Sprinkle parmesan and basil over top.

Makes 4 servings

Super Simple Pizza Dough

1 cup all-purpose flour
1 cup whole wheat flour
1 envelope (21/4 teaspoons) fast
    rising dry yeast
1/2 teaspoon salt
2/3 cup warm (115° to 125°F) water
1 tablespoon olive oil
1 tablespoon honey or sugar

Place flours, yeast, and salt in work bowl of food processor fitted with steel knife blade. In 1-cup glass measure, stir together warm water, olive oil, and honey. With machine running, pour liquid mixture through feed tube in slow steady stream; process until dough forms a ball and cleans sides of bowl. Process for 30 seconds. Let dough rest in processor bowl for 10 minutes (while preparing toppings). Shape dough as directed above.

Makes one 12-inch pizza crust

Per serving

Calories 449
Fat 17 g
Cholesterol 8 mg
Sodium 850 mg
Carbohydrate 63 g
Fiber 6 g

menus for every occasion

Dining with Family and Friends

Menu

An invitation to brunch brings the promise of relaxation and enjoying a leisurely meal with good friends. Our menu includes warm, familiar favorites that make it easy for you to host a mid-day gathering.

Come for Brunch

Beer Basted Ham	135
Overnight Blueberry French Toast	135
Cherry Almond Twist Pastry	136
Strawberry Gouda Spinach Salad	88
Assorted Juices	
Coffee and Tea	

Beer Basted Ham

A succulent glazed ham is the perfect centerpiece for your brunch table. The flavorful pan sauce keeps it moist and juicy.

1 boneless fully-cooked petite ham
    or half ham (about 5 pounds)
1 can (12 ounces) beer
1 cup firmly packed brown sugar
1/2 cup dijon-style mustard
3 tablespoons brandy, whiskey, or
    apple juice

Remove string net from ham, if necessary; place in shallow roasting pan slightly larger than ham. Pour beer over ham. Bake in 325°F oven for 1 hour, basting occasionally with pan juices. In small bowl, combine brown sugar, mustard, and brandy; spread over ham. Increase oven temperature to 425°F. Bake ham, basting twice with pan juices, until glaze browns and internal temperature is 140°F, about 20 minutes. Let stand 10 minutes before slicing. Serve with pan sauce.

Makes 16-20 servings

Per serving

Calories 224
Fat 7 g
Cholesterol 63 mg
Sodium 1542 mg
Carbohydrate 8 g
Fiber <1 g

Overnight Blueberry French Toast

Wake up to this luscious make-ahead French toast studded with plump blueberries. What a great way to start the day!

1 loaf (8 ounces) French baguette,
    cut into 1-inch slices
4 eggs
2 cups milk
1/2 cup firmly packed brown sugar
1 teaspoon ground cinnamon
1 teaspoon vanilla extract
2 cups fresh or frozen blueberries
    (do not thaw)
1/4 cup butter or margarine
1/4 cup firmly packed brown sugar
Powdered sugar (optional)

Arrange bread in single layer in greased 9×13-inch baking dish. In large bowl with hand mixer, beat eggs, milk, the 1/2 cup brown sugar, cinnamon, and vanilla. Pour mixture evenly over bread; turn slices as needed to coat completely. Cover and refrigerate overnight. Just before baking, sprinkle berries over bread. In small saucepan, heat butter with the 1/4 cup brown sugar over medium heat until bubbly. Drizzle over berries. Bake in 375°F oven until set, about 25 to 30 minutes. If desired, dust top with powdered sugar.

Makes 8 servings

Per serving

Calories 299
Fat 10 g
Cholesterol 127 mg
Sodium 280 mg
Carbohydrate 43 g
Fiber 2 g

Cherry Almond Twist Pastry

You'll be surprised how easy it is to make this very special breakfast or brunch treat. And you'll love the combination of almonds and dried cherries swirled through rich, delicate puff pastry.

1 package (3 ounces) dried cherries (about 2/3 cup)
1 package (7 to 8 ounces) almond paste (not marzipan)
1/4 cup butter, softened
1 box (17.3 ounces) frozen puff pastry sheets, thawed
1 egg, beaten with 1 teaspoon water
1/4 cup sliced almonds (optional)

Place dried cherries in small bowl with just enough hot water to cover. Let stand for 3 to 5 minutes. Drain; set aside. In work bowl of food processor fitted with steel knife blade, process almond paste and butter until smooth. Add cherries; pulse just until cherries are evenly mixed (cherries should still be chunky).

On lightly floured surface, roll one of the pastry sheets into 11-inch square. Place on parchment-lined baking sheet. With sharp knife or pizza cutter, trim corners to form 11-inch circle. Spread almond filling evenly over pastry, leaving 1/2-inch border around edges. Roll second sheet of pastry into 11-inch square. Place over filling. Trim to fit bottom layer; seal edges. Lightly press 11/2-inch round biscuit cutter in center of pastry to form guideline. Cut pastry into 16 equal wedges, cutting just to edge of center circle. (Wedges should be about 11/2 inches wide at outside edge.) Give each wedge a double twist, forming starburst pattern. Brush egg mixture over pastry. If desired, sprinkle almonds over top. Bake in 400°F oven until pastry is golden brown and puffed, about 20 minutes. Cool slightly. Best served warm.

Makes 8-10 servings

Per serving

Calories 439
Fat 30 g
Cholesterol 34 mg
Sodium 168 mg
Carbohydrate 38 g
Fiber 2 g

Menu

The gracious appeal of a ladies' luncheon is timeless. It's the perfect way to honor the bride-to-be, celebrate a birthday, or just catch up with friends.

Ladies Who Lunch

Lemon Blueberry Tea Bread

Plenty of fresh lemon zest and plump blueberries makes this delicate tea bread a special treat. Enjoy a slice with a cup of tea, a good friend, or both!

1¹/₂ cups flour

1 teaspoon baking powder

¹/₄ teaspoon salt

1 teaspoon grated lemon peel

6 tablespoons butter, softened

1 cup sugar

1 tablespoon fresh lemon juice

2 eggs, slightly beaten

¹/₂ cup milk

¹/₂ cup fresh or frozen blueberries
(do not thaw)

Lemon Glaze (recipe follows)

In medium bowl, whisk together flour, baking powder, and salt. Stir in lemon peel; set aside. In large mixer bowl, beat together butter, sugar, and lemon juice at medium speed until mixture holds together. Add eggs; beat until very light and fluffy. With mixer at low speed, add ¹/₄ of flour mixture alternately with ¹/₃ of milk (beginning and ending with flour mixture), beating after each addition just until combined. Stir in blueberries. Pour batter into 9×5-inch loaf pan that has been coated with no-stick cooking spray. Smooth top. Bake in 325°F oven until wooden pick inserted in center comes out clean, about 60 to 65 minutes. Cool bread in pan for 10 minutes. Remove from pan and place upright on wire rack. Using thin skewer, pierce entire surface of bread. Brush lemon glaze over top until all glaze is absorbed. Cool completely.

Makes 1 loaf

TIP Batter may be divided among three 3×5-inch mini-loaf pans. Bake for 50 to 55 minutes.

Lemon Glaze

¹/₄ cup sugar

3 tablespoons fresh lemon juice

Combine sugar and lemon juice in 2-cup glass measure. Microwave (high) for 30 to 45 seconds. Stir until sugar is completely dissolved.

Makes ¹/₄ cup

Per ¹/2-inch-thick slice

Calories 157

Fat 6 g

Cholesterol 39 mg

Sodium 106 mg

Carbohydrate 25 g

Fiber 1 g

Photograph on page 141

Toasted Pecan Chicken Salad

Creamy chicken salad is the quintessential luncheon entrée. Try all three tempting variations.

1 whole roasted chicken
   (about 2 pounds)
3/4 cup coarsely chopped celery
3/4 cup seedless red grapes, halved
3/4 cup pecan pieces, toasted
3/4 cup mayonnaise
2 tablespoons milk
1 teaspoon dried parsley flakes
Salt and pepper to taste

Remove meat from chicken; shred into bite-sized pieces (about 3 cups). In large bowl, combine chicken, celery, grapes, and pecans. In small bowl, stir together mayonnaise, milk, parsley, salt, and pepper. Gently stir mayonnaise mixture into chicken mixture until well combined. Chill before serving on bed of lettuce.

Makes 4-6 servings

TIP For convenience and excellent flavor, use a rotisserie chicken from Dierbergs Deli.

Hawaiian Chicken Salad

Omit grapes and pecans. Add 1 can (8 ounces) pineapple tidbits, drained; and 3/4 cup toasted almonds or macadamia nuts.

Per serving
Calories 453; Fat 36 g; Cholesterol 73 mg; Sodium 237 mg; Carbohydrate 8 g; Fiber 3 g

Waldorf Chicken Salad

Omit grapes and pecans. Add 1 medium apple, cored and chopped; and 3/4 cup toasted walnuts. Stir 1/2 teaspoon curry powder into mayonnaise mixture before adding to chicken.

Per serving
Calories 453; Fat 37 g; Cholesterol 73 mg; Sodium 232 mg; Carbohydrate 6 g; Fiber 1 g

Per serving

Calories 437
Fat 37 g
Cholesterol 73 mg
Sodium 232 mg
Carbohydrate 5 g
Fiber 2 g

Recipe for Lemon Blueberry Tea Bread (pictured) on page 139

Menu

*Rediscover the simple pleasure of gathering
the family around the dinner table.
Roasted chicken and potatoes get a delicious
makeover that will have everyone asking
for second helpings.*

Sunday Dinner at Home

Lemon and Herb Roasted Chicken

The elegant simplicity of roasted chicken makes a perfect entrée for so many occasions.

1 whole roasting chicken
(about 6 to 8 pounds)
1 bunch fresh Italian parsley
1 lemon
1 package (3/4 ounce) fresh thyme
3 tablespoons olive oil
1/2 teaspoon salt
1/4 teaspoon ground black pepper
3 cloves garlic, unpeeled
1 bag (24 ounces) baby potatoes,
halved if large
1/2 pound baby carrots
6 shallots, halved if large
12 baby red onions
3 tablespoons flour
1 cup chicken broth

Remove and discard giblets from chicken cavity. Use fingers to gently separate skin from breast meat. Arrange several parsley leaves under skin, smoothing into place. Use wooden picks to secure skin over breast meat to prevent shrinkage during roasting. Place chicken in bottom of broiler pan that has been coated with no-stick cooking spray.

Grate peel from lemon (about 2 teaspoons). Strip 1 tablespoon thyme leaves from stems. In small bowl, combine olive oil, lemon peel, thyme, salt, and pepper. Brush some of the mixture over entire surface of chicken. Cut lemon in half; gently squeeze both halves over chicken. Place remaining lemon halves inside chicken cavity along with garlic, 2 large sprigs parsley, and several sprigs fresh thyme. Roast in 375°F oven for 1 1/2 hours, basting occasionally with oil mixture. Remove from oven. Add vegetables to pan alongside chicken. Toss vegetables to coat with pan drippings. Roast until vegetables are tender, turning vegetables and basting chicken twice with any remaining oil mixture or pan juices, about 30 minutes. Remove vegetables from roasting pan; keep warm. Continue roasting chicken until internal temperature of breast meat is 170°F. Let stand tented with foil for 10 minutes before carving.

Skim fat from pan drippings. Place pan with drippings over medium heat; stir to scrape browned bits from bottom of pan. In small bowl, dissolve flour in chicken broth. Add to pan drippings. Cook over medium heat until mixture begins to boil and thicken. Serve with chicken.

Photograph on book jacket
and page 2

Makes 6-8 servings

**Per 3-ounce serving
(skinless breast meat)
with vegetables**

Calories 182
Fat 3 g
Cholesterol 32 mg
Sodium 323 mg
Carbohydrate 23 g
Fiber 3 g

**Per serving (dark meat)
with vegetables**

Calories 276
Fat 12 g
Cholesterol 69 mg
Sodium 347 mg
Carbohydrate 23 g
Fiber 3 g

Apple Jack Tart

Jack Daniel's adds a splash of fun to a classic fall dessert. The pretty lattice top is simple to weave and gives this spirited tart a pastry-shop look.

1 package (15 ounces) refrigerated
    pie crust
1/2 cup sweetened dried cranberries
3 tablespoons Jack Daniel's whiskey
1/2 cup granulated sugar
1 tablespoon flour
1/2 teaspoon ground cinnamon
1/2 teaspoon ground ginger
4 cups peeled, cored, and thinly
    sliced apples (Braeburn,
    Jonathan, or Granny Smith)

GLAZE
1/4 cup powdered sugar
2 to 3 teaspoons Jack Daniel's
    whiskey

Place baking sheet in 400°F oven. Place one of the pie crusts in 10-inch tart pan with removable bottom. Fold in excess dough and press around edges and onto bottom of pan. In large bowl, combine dried cranberries and the 3 tablespoons whiskey. In small bowl, combine sugar, flour, and spices. Add apples and sugar mixture to cranberries; toss until well combined. Arrange fruit mixture in tart pan. On lightly floured surface, roll second pie crust to smooth creases; cut into 1/2-inch strips. Arrange strips in lattice pattern over apples. Trim and seal edges. Place on preheated baking sheet. Bake until filling is bubbly and crust is golden brown, about 40 to 45 minutes. Remove pan from baking sheet; cool on wire rack for 15 minutes. In small bowl, stir together glaze ingredients. Drizzle over tart. Remove sides of pan; cool completely.

Makes 8 servings

TIP If tart pan is not available, use 9-inch pie plate.

Per serving

Calories 371
Fat 14 g
Cholesterol 10 mg
Sodium 198 mg
Carbohydrate 56 g
Fiber 1 g

Menu

Whether it's the first chilly night of the season or winter is well under way, this comforting meal is the perfect way to entertain a crowd on a lazy weekend. Fireplace not required!

Cozy Fireside Dinner

Roasted Eye of Round

This is a roast you'll want to serve time and again throughout the year. It will soon become a family favorite.

1 eye of round beef roast
    (about 3 pounds)
2 tablespoons vegetable oil (divided)
1 can (14 ounces) beef broth
1/2 cup dry red wine
2 tablespoons Worcestershire sauce
1 cup finely chopped onion
1 clove garlic, minced
2 tablespoons flour
2 tablespoons tomato paste
1/4 teaspoon salt
1/4 teaspoon ground black pepper

Trim visible fat from beef. In Dutch oven, heat 1 tablespoon of the oil over medium-high heat. Add roast; cook until browned on all sides. In 4-cup glass measure, combine broth, wine, and Worcestershire sauce. Pour over beef. Cover and cook in 325°F oven until well done and tender, about 2 1/4 to 2 1/2 hours. Remove beef from pan, reserving liquid. In large skillet over medium-high heat, heat remaining 1 tablespoon oil. Add onion and garlic; cook until soft, about 4 minutes. Stir in flour and cook for 1 minute. Gradually stir in reserved liquid; bring to a boil. Cook, stirring constantly until thickened. Stir in tomato paste, salt, and pepper. Cook, stirring occasionally until thickened. Slice beef across the grain. Serve with sauce.

Makes 12 servings

Per 3-ounce cooked portion

Calories 196
Fat 10 g
Cholesterol 41 mg
Sodium 235 mg
Carbohydrate 3 g
Fiber <1 g

Pumpkin Cheesecake Bars

The combination of pumpkin pie and cheesecake is simply irresistible. And when dessert is this easy to make, who needs a special occasion?

1 package (18 ounces) refrigerated ready-to-bake sugar cookie dough

1 package (10 ounces) cinnamon-flavored baking chips

3 packages (8 ounces each) cream cheese, softened

3/4 cup sugar

1 teaspoon vanilla extract

1 cup pure pumpkin

1 teaspoon pumpkin pie spice

3 eggs

Arrange 15 of the cookie dough pieces in greased 9×13-inch baking pan; pat out to cover bottom of pan. (Reserve remaining dough for another use.) Sprinkle chips over dough. Bake in 350°F oven until crust is lightly browned, about 12 to 14 minutes. In large mixer bowl, beat cream cheese, sugar, and vanilla at medium speed until smooth. Add pumpkin and spice; beat at low speed until blended. Beat in eggs. Pour batter over crust. Bake until center is set, about 30 to 35 minutes. Cool in pan on wire rack to room temperature. Chill for several hours before cutting into squares.

Makes 18 bars

TIP If cinnamon chips are not available, substitute butterscotch chips or white baking chips.

Per bar

Calories 388

Fat 24 g

Cholesterol 85 mg

Sodium 281 mg

Carbohydrate 36 g

Fiber 1 g

Menu

Capture the taste of Italy in this menu filled with simple dishes and big, bold flavors. Chicken Spiedini is one of our most requested recipes.

Italian Country Dinner

Chicken Spiedini

These lightly breaded chicken spirals never fail to get rave reviews. A swirl of lemon and garlic makes them irresistible.

4 boneless, skinless chicken breast halves (about 1 pound)

2/3 cup Italian seasoned bread crumbs

1/3 cup grated parmesan cheese

1 tablespoon chopped fresh Italian parsley

2 teaspoons grated lemon peel

2 cloves garlic, minced

2 tablespoons butter or margarine, melted

2 tablespoons olive oil

Place chicken between 2 sheets of plastic wrap; pound lightly until very thin (about 1/4 inch thick). On waxed paper, combine bread crumbs, cheese, parsley, lemon peel, and garlic. In shallow dish, combine butter and olive oil. Dip each piece of chicken into butter mixture; coat both sides with crumb mixture. Tightly roll up each piece. Cut into 1-inch-thick slices; thread onto skewers. Place skewers on oiled grid over medium-high heat; grill until chicken is cooked through and coating is lightly browned, about 5 minutes per side.

Makes 4 servings

TO BROIL Place skewers on rack of broiler pan that has been coated with no-stick cooking spray. Broil for 4 to 5 minutes per side.

Grilled Beef Spiedini

Use 1 pound beef breakfast steaks (thinly sliced top round) instead of chicken. Proceed with above directions.

Per serving with chicken

Calories 298

Fat 16 g

Cholesterol 65 mg

Sodium 708 mg

Carbohydrate 15 g

Fiber 1 g

Per serving with beef

Calories 348

Fat 19 g

Cholesterol 79 mg

Sodium 715 mg

Carbohydrate 15 g

Fiber 1 g

Recipe for Garden Risotto
(pictured) on page 94

Lemon Berry Tiramisu

This version of Italy's famous dessert showcases fresh berries in a refreshing lemon cream surrounded by delicate ladyfingers.

2 packages (3 ounces each) frozen
    ladyfingers, thawed (divided)
1/2 cup berry liqueur (Chambord)
1 can (15 3/4 ounces) lemon pie filling
1 container (15 ounces) ricotta
    cheese
1 cup powdered sugar
1 teaspoon vanilla extract
1 cup heavy whipping cream,
    whipped
2 cups fresh blueberries (divided)
1 cup fresh raspberries

Brush flat side of ladyfingers with liqueur. Trim one end from half of the ladyfingers to make straight edge; use to line sides of 9-inch springform pan. Use trimmings and additional ladyfingers to cover bottom of pan. In large mixer bowl, beat pie filling, ricotta, powdered sugar, and vanilla at medium speed until light and fluffy. Fold in whipped cream. Spread half of the lemon mixture into pan and top with half of the blueberries. Repeat layers with remaining ladyfingers and lemon mixture. Cover and refrigerate several hours or overnight. Just before serving, top with remaining blueberries and raspberries.

Makes 12 servings

TIP If desired, use raspberry syrup or melted seedless raspberry jam in place of liqueur.

Per serving

Calories 281
Fat 11 g
Cholesterol 48 mg
Sodium 182 mg
Carbohydrate 39 g
Fiber 2 g

Menu

Barbecue in St. Louis means one thing—pork steaks—with the occasional slab of ribs just for fun. And be sure to have the large paper plates—you'll need room for all of the delicious sides.

St. Louis-Style BBQ

Oh, Baby! Barbecued Ribs

Here's how to make tender, juicy, and absolutely delicious barbecued ribs.

3 slabs (about 1 1/2 pounds each) pork loin back ribs (baby backs), or 2 to 3 slabs (about 2 pounds each) pork spare ribs

2 cups Two-Brew Barbecue Sauce (recipe follows)

Slide sharp knife under membrane covering back of ribs to loosen. Grasp firmly with paper towel and remove. Place each slab of ribs on double thickness of heavy-duty foil. Sprinkle each with 2 tablespoons water. Fold to form tightly sealed packet, allowing space for steam. Place on grid over medium heat; grill for 45 minutes, turning occasionally. Remove ribs from foil. Place ribs directly on grid over medium heat; grill for 45 minutes, turning occasionally and basting with sauce during last 20 minutes.

Makes 4-6 servings

Per serving with sauce

Calories 643
Fat 44 g
Cholesterol 165 mg
Sodium 702 mg
Carbohydrate 22 g
Fiber 1 g

St. Louis-Style Pork Steaks

Tender pork steaks slathered in sweet and tangy sauce are a barbecue staple.

4 center-cut pork steaks (about 3 pounds)

1 cup Two-Brew Barbecue Sauce (recipe follows)

Place pork steaks on grid over medium heat; grill for 30 to 35 minutes, turning occasionally and basting with sauce during last 10 minutes.

Makes 4-6 servings

Per serving with sauce

Calories 398
Fat 24 g
Cholesterol 119 mg
Sodium 378 mg
Carbohydrate 11 g
Fiber <1 g

Two-Brew Barbecue Sauce

2 cups ketchup
1/2 cup beer or apple juice
1/2 cup strong brewed coffee
1/2 cup honey
2 tablespoons Worcestershire sauce
2 teaspoons chili powder
1 teaspoon ground cumin
Salt and pepper to taste

In medium saucepan, combine all ingredients. Bring to a boil over medium-high heat. Reduce heat, cover, and simmer for 10 minutes or until slightly thickened. Use as a basting sauce on pork or chicken. Store sauce in refrigerator.

Makes 3 1/2 cups

Per 2 tablespoons

Calories 38
Fat <1 g
Cholesterol 0 mg
Sodium 247 mg
Carbohydrate 10 g
Fiber <1 g

Mint Chip Ice Cream Pie

Inspired by a favorite cookie—you know the one—this cool and frosty pie is a great way to cool off after a spicy barbecue, or any time!

15 mint cream-filled chocolate
    sandwich cookies
3 tablespoons butter, melted
1 cup miniature marshmallows
1 cup (6 ounces) semi-sweet
    chocolate chips
1/3 cup milk
1/2 gallon mint chip ice cream

In work bowl of food processor fitted with steel knife blade, process cookies to form crumbs. Add butter; process until evenly mixed. Press crumb mixture on bottom and up sides of 9-inch pie plate. In medium microwave-safe bowl, combine marshmallows, chocolate chips, and milk. Microwave (high) for 1 minute; stir. Microwave in 30-second intervals until melted and smooth. Pour half of fudge sauce over cookie crust; freeze for 30 minutes. Refrigerate remaining sauce in microwave-safe container. Cut ice cream into 1/2-inch-thick slices; fit into crust, pressing and smoothing as desired. Freeze several hours or overnight. Place reserved sauce in microwave. Microwave (high) for 45 seconds. Cut pie into wedges with knife dipped in hot water. Serve with warm fudge sauce.

Makes 8-10 servings

Per serving

Calories 520
Fat 28 g
Cholesterol 50 mg
Sodium 218 mg
Carbohydrate 60 g
Fiber 1 g

Menu

Why not indulge that special someone—or yourself—in this sophisticated supper. The luxurious lobster pasta is simply unforgettable!

Candlelight Dinner

Lobster Capellini

Sweet, succulent lobster in a rich gruyère sauce is nothing less than luxurious. Add the company of very special friends for a memorable evening.

1½ pounds frozen slipper lobster
    tails (about 6), thawed
1 cup dry white wine
½ teaspoon ground white pepper
½ pound shiitake mushrooms,
    stemmed and caps sliced
2 large cloves garlic, minced
2 tablespoons butter
2 tablespoons cornstarch, dissolved
    in 2 tablespoons water
2 cups heavy whipping cream
8 ounces gruyère cheese, shredded
    (about 2 cups)
Hot cooked angel hair (capellini)
    pasta or linguine
Snipped fresh chives (optional)

Remove lobster meat from shell. In medium saucepan, bring wine and pepper to a boil over medium-high heat. Place lobster meat and shells in wine; cover and cook until lobster is opaque, about 5 minutes. Remove lobster meat from wine; reserve wine. Cut lobster meat into chunks; set aside. In medium skillet, cook mushrooms and garlic in butter over medium-high heat until mushrooms are tender. Strain wine into skillet; discard shells. Stir in cornstarch mixture and cream; bring to a boil and cook for 2 minutes. Remove from heat. Stir in lobster meat and cheese; stir until cheese is melted. Serve over pasta. If desired, garnish with chives.

Makes 4-6 servings

Per serving without pasta

Calories 592
Fat 46 g
Cholesterol 185 mg
Sodium 250 mg
Carbohydrate 6 g
Fiber <1 g

Baklava Sundaes

Capture the flavors of the classic Greek pastry in this simple yet elegant dessert.

12 sheets (about 1/2 of 16-ounce
    twin package) frozen fillo dough,
    thawed in refrigerator overnight
1/3 cup butter, melted
Vanilla ice cream
Honey-Nut Sauce (recipe follows)

Place 12 sheets of fillo on work surface; cover completely with plastic wrap. Rewrap and refreeze remaining fillo for other uses. Place 1 sheet fillo on clean dry surface; brush with butter. Top with 5 more fillo sheets, brushing each sheet with butter. Cut stack of fillo into six 4-inch squares. Form 6 cups by pressing squares into muffin cups; corners should extend above edges of pan. Repeat with remaining 6 sheets of fillo and butter. Bake in 375°F oven until golden brown, about 5 to 6 minutes. Cool in pan on wire rack. To serve, spoon ice cream into baked cups. Top with Honey-Nut Sauce.

Makes 12 servings

Honey-Nut Sauce

1/2 cup sugar
1/2 cup water
1 cup chopped walnuts, toasted
1/2 cup honey
1 teaspoon grated lemon peel
2 teaspoons fresh lemon juice

In medium saucepan, bring sugar and water to a boil over medium-high heat. Reduce heat and simmer for 5 minutes. Remove from heat; stir in remaining ingredients. Cool to room temperature before spooning over ice cream-filled cups.

Makes 2 cups

**Per serving with
1/2 cup vanilla ice cream
and 2 tablespoons sauce**

Calories 344
Fat 19 g
Cholesterol 43 mg
Sodium 183 mg
Carbohydrate 41 g
Fiber 1 g

Menu

A new job, an engagement, birthday best wishes—life is full of reasons to celebrate! Treat the guest of honor to a meal that's just as special as the occasion itself.

Let's Celebrate

Pork Tenderloin with Orange Rosemary Sauce

Slivers of garlic and orange peel nestled inside the tenderloin give it a subtle flavor. Prepare the orange butter ahead so the flavors have time to blend.

2 pork tenderloins
(about 1¼ pounds each)
2 large cloves garlic, cut into slivers
8 thin strips fresh orange peel,
about 1 inch long
½ cup butter, softened
2 tablespoons frozen orange juice
concentrate, thawed
1 tablespoon grated orange peel
1 tablespoon finely chopped fresh
rosemary, or 2 teaspoons dried
rosemary, crushed
Salt and pepper to taste
1 cup chicken broth

Trim fat and silver skin from tenderloins. With sharp knife, make 8 small, deep slits in each tenderloin. Alternately insert garlic slivers and strips of orange peel into slits. In small bowl, combine butter, orange juice concentrate, grated orange peel, and rosemary.

In medium skillet, melt 2 tablespoons of the orange butter over medium-high heat. Add tenderloins; cook until browned on all sides, about 5 to 7 minutes. Place tenderloins on rack in shallow roasting pan. Season meat generously with salt and pepper. Pour skillet drippings over top; set skillet aside. Spread additional 1 teaspoon orange butter over each tenderloin. Pour broth into pan. Roast in 350°F oven until internal temperature is 155°F, about 25 to 30 minutes. Place pork on serving platter; tent with foil to keep warm.

Return pan drippings to skillet. Bring to a boil over medium-high heat; cook until reduced by one-half. Whisk in remaining orange butter. Cook, stirring constantly for 1½ to 2 minutes. Slice pork and arrange on serving platter. Drizzle sauce over top.

Makes 8-10 servings

Per serving

Calories 240
Fat 15 g
Cholesterol 97 mg
Sodium 210 mg
Carbohydrate 2 g
Fiber <1 g

White Chocolate Mousse Torte

This impressive no-bake torte is simple to make and heavenly to eat. Adorn the torte with a festive ribbon for presentation. Remove the ribbon just before serving.

1 can (14.1 ounces) chocolate-filled
   pirouette cookies
3 cups (18 ounces) white
   baking chips
2 packages (8 ounces each) cream
   cheese, softened
1/4 to 1/3 cup liqueur (see tip)
2 tablespoons honey
2 cups heavy whipping cream,
   whipped
Grated semi-sweet chocolate
   (optional)

Using serrated knife, carefully cut cookies into 3-inch pieces. Stand cookies around inside edge of 8-inch springform pan. Crush trim pieces and enough remaining cookies to make 1 cup crumbs; spread in bottom of pan. Place white baking chips in medium microwave-safe bowl. Microwave (high) and stir in 30-second intervals, until chips are melted. With hand mixer, beat in cream cheese, liqueur, and honey until smooth. Gently fold in whipped cream. Carefully pour mixture into center of prepared springform pan; spread and smooth top. Cover and refrigerate for at least 6 hours before serving. (If desired, freeze torte for up to 1 month. Filling will have an ice cream-like consistency when served frozen.) If desired, garnish top with grated chocolate.

Makes 16 servings

TIP Try any of these flavors: almond (Amaretto); hazelnut (Frangelico); coffee (Kahlúa, Tía Maria).

Per serving

Calories 553
Fat 37 g
Cholesterol 79 mg
Sodium 193 mg
Carbohydrate 46 g
Fiber 0 g

Menu

Candles are aglow, the silver is sparkling—
this is the dinner you've waited for all
year long. Our Standing Rib Roast takes
center stage in this sumptuous meal that
guests will long remember.

A Splendid Holiday Feast

Cranberry Topped Brie	18
Boston Lettuce with Crumbled Blue Cheese Dressing	86
Standing Rib Roast	165
Horseradish Mashed Potatoes	100
Glazed Carrots	97
Chambord Cream Cake Roll	166

Standing Rib Roast

This impressive cut of beef is crowned the "king of roasts." But don't be intimidated. It's actually very simple to prepare!

1 beef rib roast (6 to 8 pounds),
   chine bone removed
1 tablespoon Italian herb seasoning
10 cloves garlic
2 cups dry red wine
1 teaspoon coarse salt
1/2 teaspoon cracked black pepper

Place roast, fat-side up, on rack of broiler pan. Rub surface of meat with Italian seasoning. Roast in 350°F oven until internal temperature is 150°F for medium, about 2 1/2 to 3 hours. During last hour of roasting, tuck garlic under meat so it is completely covered. Remove roast and rack from pan. Cover meat and let stand for 15 minutes. Place pan with drippings over medium-high heat. Add wine, salt, and pepper; stir to scrape browned bits from bottom of pan. Cook until reduced by one-half, about 10 minutes. Skim fat from sauce. Slice beef and serve with pan sauce.

Makes 8-10 servings

To Carve a Beef Rib Roast

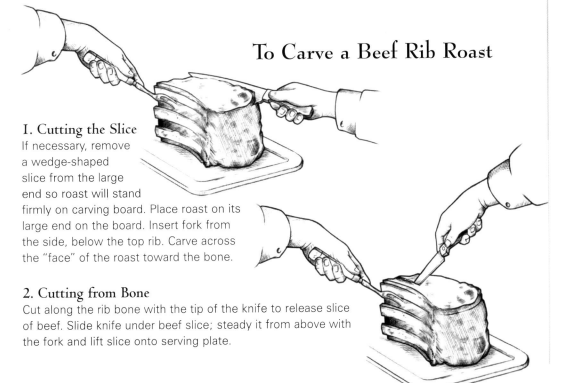

1. Cutting the Slice

If necessary, remove a wedge-shaped slice from the large end so roast will stand firmly on carving board. Place roast on its large end on the board. Insert fork from the side, below the top rib. Carve across the "face" of the roast toward the bone.

2. Cutting from Bone

Cut along the rib bone with the tip of the knife to release slice of beef. Slide knife under beef slice; steady it from above with the fork and lift slice onto serving plate.

Per serving

Calories 288
Fat 11 g
Cholesterol 81 mg
Sodium 282 mg
Carbohydrate 2 g
Fiber <1 g

Per 3-ounce cooked portion

Calories 192
Fat 7 g
Cholesterol 54 mg
Sodium 188 mg
Carbohydrate 2 g
Fiber <1 g

Chambord Cream Cake Roll

Keep this beautiful cake roll on-hand in your freezer. Raspberry liqueur adds elegant sweetness to the filling and sauce.

4 eggs, at room temperature
3/4 cup granulated sugar
1 tablespoon vegetable oil
1 teaspoon vanilla extract
2/3 cup flour
1 teaspoon baking powder
1/4 teaspoon salt
Powdered sugar

FILLING
1 cup heavy whipping cream
1/4 cup powdered sugar
Chambord Berry Sauce (divided)
   (recipe follows)
2 tablespoons berry liqueur
   (Chambord)

Lightly coat bottom and sides of 10×15-inch jellyroll pan with no-stick cooking spray. Line with parchment paper; spray parchment and set aside. In large mixer bowl, beat eggs and granulated sugar at high speed for 5 minutes (7 minutes with hand mixer) until very thick and pale. Stir in oil and vanilla. In small bowl, whisk together flour, baking powder, and salt. Sprinkle over egg mixture; fold in until well combined. Spread evenly into prepared pan. Bake in 350°F oven until lightly browned and sides begin to pull away from edges, about 10 to 12 minutes. Sprinkle powdered sugar over cake and clean cloth towel. Place towel, sugared-side down, on top of cake. Place large cutting board on top and invert cake onto towel. Remove parchment. Starting at one short side, gently roll up cake with towel. Let stand for 15 minutes.

FOR FILLING In large chilled mixer bowl, beat cream, the 1/4 cup powdered sugar, 2 tablespoons of the Berry Sauce, and liqueur at low speed until well blended. Beat at high speed until stiff peaks form. Gently unroll cake. Spread 1/2 cup of the Berry Sauce over cake. Spread filling evenly over cake, leaving 1-inch border on short ends. Using towel as aid, gently roll cake with filling, lifting as you roll to keep filling in place. Place cake roll, seam-side down, on sheet of plastic wrap; completely enclose cake in wrap. Freeze at least 2 hours.

Per serving with 2 tablespoons sauce

Calories 339
Fat 16 g
Cholesterol 147 mg
Sodium 172 mg
Carbohydrate 46 g
Fiber 2 g

Photograph on page 168

Powdered sugar
Sugared Cranberries & Rosemary
   (optional) (recipe follows)

TO SERVE Trim ends from cake. Dust top generously with powdered sugar. Place on serving platter. If desired, garnish with Sugared Cranberries and Rosemary. Slice and serve with remaining berry sauce.

Makes 8 servings

TIP For best cake volume, place eggs in shell in bowl of very warm tap water for 10 minutes before beating.

Chambord Berry Sauce

1¹/₂ cups fresh or frozen cranberries
   (do not thaw)
1 bag (12 ounces) frozen
   blackberries, partially thawed
²/₃ cup granulated sugar
2 tablespoons berry liqueur
   (Chambord)

Place cranberries in microwave-safe bowl; cover and microwave (high) for 2 minutes or until berries pop. In work bowl of food processor fitted with steel knife blade or in blender container, combine cranberries, blackberries, and sugar. Purée until smooth. Strain; discard seeds. Stir in liqueur. Chill.

Makes 2 cups

Sugared Cranberries & Rosemary

In small bowl, combine 2 tablespoons powdered sugar and 1 tablespoon water. Dip cranberries and rosemary sprigs in mixture. Roll berries in granulated sugar until lightly coated; sprinkle granulated sugar over rosemary. Gently shake to remove excess sugar. Place on waxed paper until dried. Use as garnish.

Menu

Share this wonderful meal with very special friends. From the luscious Beef Tenderloin Napoleon to the silky White Russian Crème Brûlée, you'll savor every bite.

Stylish Supper for Four

Recipe for Chambord Cream Cake Roll
(pictured) on page 166

Beef Tenderloin Napoleon with Wild Mushrooms and Red Wine Sauce

Dazzle your dinner guests with this fabulous entrée. Preparing the Red Wine Sauce a day ahead enhances its rich flavor.

1 sheet (1/2 of 17.3-ounce box) frozen puff pastry, thawed
1 egg, beaten with 1 tablespoon water
1 pound center-cut beef tenderloin
2 tablespoons olive oil (divided)
2 teaspoons dried thyme
4 ounces shiitake mushrooms
4 ounces baby portabella mushrooms
1 tablespoon butter
1 large shallot, diced
1 large clove garlic, minced
1/4 teaspoon salt
1/8 teaspoon ground black pepper
1/4 cup dry red wine
Red Wine Sauce (recipe follows)

On lightly floured surface, roll pastry sheet to smooth creases. Cut four 4×3-inch rectangles from pastry for bases. Cut small stars out of remaining pastry for tops. Place on parchment-lined baking sheet. Brush with egg mixture. Chill for 30 minutes. Bake in 375°F oven until golden brown and puffed, about 15 minutes. Cool on wire rack.

Rub surface of tenderloin with 1 tablespoon of the olive oil and coat with thyme. Place on rack in shallow roasting pan. Roast in 425°F oven until internal temperature is 145°F, about 35 to 40 minutes. Let stand 15 minutes.

Meanwhile, remove stems from mushrooms and reserve for Red Wine Sauce. Slice mushroom caps. In large skillet, melt butter with remaining tablespoon olive oil over medium-high heat. Add sliced mushrooms, shallot, garlic, salt, and pepper. Cook for 1 to 2 minutes. Add wine; cook, stirring occasionally until all moisture evaporates, about 10 to 12 minutes. Make Red Wine Sauce. Stir 2 tablespoons sauce into mushroom mixture.

Slice tenderloin into 4 medallions. Spoon sauce onto individual plates. On each plate, layer 1 pastry base, mushrooms, 1 beef medallion, and more sauce. Top each with pastry stars.

Makes 4 servings

Per serving with 2 tablespoons sauce

Calories 711
Fat 45 g
Cholesterol 118 mg
Sodium 598 mg
Carbohydrate 34 g
Fiber 3 g

Photograph on page 172

Red Wine Sauce

2 teaspoons olive oil

Mushroom stems (reserved from
    Beef Tenderloin Napoleon)

1 rib celery, chopped

1 carrot, chopped

1/2 medium onion, chopped

1/4 cup dry red wine

1 can (14 ounces) beef broth

2 teaspoons tomato paste

1 tablespoon butter, softened

1 tablespoon flour

In large skillet, heat oil over medium-high heat. Add mushroom stems, celery, carrot, and onion. Cook, stirring occasionally until vegetables are browned, about 8 to 10 minutes. Stir in wine; cook until reduced by one-half. Stir in broth and tomato paste. Cook until reduced to 1 cup, about 10 to 15 minutes. Strain sauce and discard vegetables. Return sauce to skillet. In small bowl, stir together butter and flour until well combined. Whisk into sauce. Cook for 5 minutes or until thickened.

Makes 1 cup

MAKE-AHEAD TIP Pastry may be baked a day ahead and stored in loosely covered container. Mushrooms may be cooked ahead and refrigerated overnight. Wine Sauce may be prepared up to the point of adding butter and flour, and refrigerated overnight. While tenderloin is roasting, microwave mushrooms for 1 to 2 minutes until warm; warm sauce and whisk in butter mixture.

White Russian Crème Brûlée

When a famous cocktail meets a classic dessert, the results are simply divine!

5 egg yolks, slightly beaten

1/3 cup sugar

3 tablespoons coffee-flavored
    liqueur (Kahlúa, Tía Maria)

2 cups half-and-half

1 teaspoon vanilla extract

4 tablespoons sugar

In medium bowl, whisk egg yolks, the 1/3 cup sugar, and liqueur until smooth. Place half-and-half in medium microwave-safe bowl. Microwave (high) for 1 to 2 minutes or until warm. Gradually whisk into yolk mixture, whisking constantly until smooth. Add vanilla. Pour into 4 ramekins; set ramekins in 9×13-inch baking pan. Remove any bubbles from surface with spoon. Pour water into baking pan to depth of 1 inch (do not allow water to splash into ramekins). Bake in 325°F oven until set, about 40 to 45 minutes. (Gently jiggle ramekins; centers should wiggle just slightly.) Remove from oven; leave ramekins in water bath for 30 minutes to continue cooking. Cover each ramekin; refrigerate at least 4 hours. Sprinkle 1 tablespoon of the remaining sugar over top of each ramekin. Place on jellyroll pan. Broil for 1 to 2 minutes to caramelize sugar; or heat sugar with kitchen torch until lightly browned. Serve immediately.

Makes 4 servings

TIP Do not substitute fat-free half-and-half.

Recipe for Beef Tenderloin Napoleon with Wild Mushrooms and Red Wine Sauce (pictured) on page 170

Per serving

Calories 367

Fat 19 g

Cholesterol 301 mg

Sodium 59 mg

Carbohydrate 38 g

Fiber 0 g

Menu

*Mixing, mingling, and sharing a wonderful
meal are what the holidays are all about.
We've dressed up comforting favorites with
some special touches, but kept preparation
simple so you can celebrate all the way
through dessert!*

Festive Holiday Buffet

Beef Brisket with Portabella Mushrooms and Dried Cherries

Red wine, portabella mushrooms, and dried cherries make the most wonderful sauce for this slow-cooked favorite. Be prepared to share the recipe!

1 flat-cut beef brisket
    (about 4 pounds)

1/4 cup flour

1 teaspoon dried oregano

1/2 teaspoon cracked black pepper

2 large onions, sliced 1/2-inch thick

1 can (14 ounces) beef broth

1 cup dry red wine

4 large cloves garlic, slivered

3 bay leaves

1 pound portabella mushrooms,
    stems and gills removed, and
    caps cut into chunks

1 package (3 ounces) dried cherries
    (about 2/3 cup)

Trim visible fat from brisket. Place in shallow roasting pan. In small bowl, combine flour, oregano, and pepper; sprinkle over top of beef. Arrange onions over top. Add broth, wine, garlic, and bay leaves to pan. Cover tightly and cook in 350°F oven for 3 1/2 hours, basting every hour. Remove brisket from pan, reserving pan sauce. Discard bay leaves. Cool beef slightly; thinly slice across the grain. Return to sauce in pan. Top with mushrooms and cherries. Cover and bake until mushrooms are tender, about 30 minutes.

Makes 8 servings

TIP Beef can be cooked, sliced, and chilled in pan sauce a day ahead. To serve, add mushrooms and cherries; increase final baking to 1 hour.

Per serving

Calories 699

Fat 47 g

Cholesterol 179 mg

Sodium 307 mg

Carbohydrate 19 g

Fiber 2 g

Triple Layer Toffee Cheesecake

Three luscious layers in one decadent cheesecake. Need we say more? Toffee is an unexpected delight amid the rich creamy layers.

CRUST

1 1/2 cups graham cracker crumbs

2 Heath candy bars (1.4 ounces each), chopped

2 tablespoons dark brown sugar

4 tablespoons butter, melted

VANILLA AND CHOCOLATE LAYERS

2 packages (8 ounces each) cream cheese, softened

1/2 cup granulated sugar

2/3 cup dairy sour cream

1 1/2 teaspoons vanilla extract

2 eggs

1/2 cup milk chocolate chips, melted and slightly cooled

TOFFEE LAYER

1 package (8 ounces) cream cheese, softened

1/4 cup firmly packed dark brown sugar

1/3 cup dairy sour cream

1 teaspoon vanilla extract

1 egg

2 Heath candy bars (1.4 ounces each), chopped

FOR CRUST In work bowl of food processor fitted with steel knife blade, combine graham cracker crumbs, chopped candy, and brown sugar; pulse to combine. Add melted butter and pulse until evenly moistened. Press mixture onto bottom and 1-inch up sides of 9-inch springform pan. Bake in 325°F oven for 6 minutes; cool.

FOR VANILLA AND CHOCOLATE LAYERS In large mixer bowl, beat cream cheese with granulated sugar at high speed until very smooth. Beat in sour cream and vanilla. Add eggs, 1 at a time, beating at low speed just until blended. Reserve 1 1/2 cups batter for vanilla layer. Blend melted chocolate into remaining batter. Spread chocolate batter over prepared crust. Bake in 325°F oven for 15 minutes (filling will be only partially set).

FOR TOFFEE LAYER While chocolate layer bakes, beat cream cheese with brown sugar in large mixer bowl until very smooth. Beat in sour cream and vanilla. Add egg, beating at low speed just until smooth (do not overmix). Stir in chopped candy. Gently spoon toffee batter over partially baked chocolate layer, spreading from edges toward center. Bake for 15 minutes.

Per serving

Calories 418

Fat 29 g

Cholesterol 105 mg

Sodium 265 mg

Carbohydrate 33 g

Fiber 1 g

GARNISH

Sweetened whipped cream

2 Heath candy bars (1.4 ounces each), chopped

Gently spoon reserved vanilla batter over partially baked toffee layer, spreading from edges toward center. Bake until entire top appears set (center will still be slightly jiggly), about 30 to 40 minutes. Turn off oven. Loosen edges of cake from pan with sharp knife. Leave cheesecake in oven with door ajar for 30 minutes. Remove from oven. Cool on wire rack to room temperature. Cover and chill overnight before removing springform ring. Garnish with sweetened whipped cream and additional chopped candy.

Makes 16 servings

TIP Coarsely chopped Heath bars are very attractive in this recipe. For convenience, you may substitute 1/4 cup milk chocolate toffee bits for each Heath bar, if desired.

from simple to sublime

Desserts to Remember

Apple Blackberry Crunch à la Mode

Tart, crisp apples and tangy blackberries are nestled beneath a sweet, crunchy topping for a warm and homey dessert. A scoop of vanilla ice cream makes it complete.

contributed by

Denise Hall

A Home Economist and former School of Cooking Manager, Denise has been teaching cooking classes since 1980. Denise was raised in Portland, Oregon, and lived in France while attending college and studying cooking. French cuisine remains her favorite but she also enjoys preparing foods indigenous to the Pacific Northwest, like crisp apples and tangy blackberries. Denise teaches Couples Cook classes with her husband, David, and enjoys sharing the history and culture of the recipes she prepares.

4 cups peeled and thinly sliced tart apples (Granny Smith, Braeburn, Jonathan) (about 4 to 5 apples)

2 cups fresh or frozen blackberries (do not thaw)

SYRUP

1 cup granulated sugar

1 cup cold water

1 tablespoon cornstarch

1 teaspoon vanilla extract

TOPPING

1 cup flour

1 cup firmly packed brown sugar

3/4 cup old-fashioned or quick-cooking rolled oats

1/2 cup butter, melted

1/2 cup chopped walnuts

1 teaspoon ground cinnamon

Place sliced apples in greased 9×13-inch baking dish. Top with berries. In small saucepan, combine all syrup ingredients. Cook over medium heat until clear. Pour hot syrup over fruit. In medium bowl, stir together all topping ingredients until crumbly. Spoon over fruit mixture. Bake in 350°F oven until top is brown and fruit is bubbling, about 1 hour. Serve warm with vanilla ice cream.

Makes 8-10 servings

Per serving with 1/4 cup vanilla ice cream

Calories 465

Fat 18 g

Cholesterol 40 mg

Sodium 106 mg

Carbohydrate 74 g

Fiber 4 g

Pumpkin Bread Pudding

The warm, cozy flavors of pumpkin pie and the old-fashioned goodness of bread pudding make a truly comforting dessert. Finish it with a drizzle of Bourbon Praline Sauce.

Perfect Whipped Cream

For perfect whipped cream, start with a deep, narrow bowl and beaters that have been chilled icy cold. Beat at low speed and gradually increase to high speed as it thickens. For the greatest volume, add sugar or flavorings after the cream forms soft peaks. To avoid overbeating, finish whisking the cream by hand until desired consistency. Once whipped, store covered in the refrigerator up to 24 hours.

Per serving with sauce and without whipped cream

Calories 413
Fat 20 g
Cholesterol 102 mg
Sodium 426 mg
Carbohydrate 50 g
Fiber 3 g

10 cups cubed country white bread
 (about 18 ounces)
3 eggs
1 can (15 ounces) pure pumpkin
1 1/2 cups milk
1 cup heavy whipping cream
3/4 cup firmly packed dark
 brown sugar
2 teaspoons vanilla extract
1 1/2 teaspoons ground cinnamon
1/8 teaspoon ground nutmeg
Dash salt
Sweetened whipped cream
Bourbon Praline Sauce
 (recipe follows)

Layer half of bread cubes in 9×13-inch baking dish that has been coated with no-stick cooking spray. Combine remaining ingredients except whipped cream and sauce in medium bowl; whisk until well blended. Pour half of pumpkin mixture over bread cubes. Repeat layers with remaining bread cubes and pumpkin mixture. Let stand for 20 to 30 minutes for bread to absorb moisture, pressing occasionally on bread to evenly moisten. Bake in 350°F oven until wooden pick inserted in center comes out clean, about 45 to 50 minutes. Cool slightly. Serve warm with dollop of whipped cream and Bourbon Praline Sauce.

Makes 12 servings

Bourbon Praline Sauce

1/2 cup pecan pieces
2 tablespoons butter
1/2 cup firmly packed dark
 brown sugar
1/2 cup heavy whipping cream
2 tablespoons bourbon

In small saucepan, combine pecan pieces and butter. Cook over medium heat, stirring frequently, until pecans are very fragrant and lightly browned, about 4 minutes. Add brown sugar and cream; bring to a boil. Reduce heat and simmer until sugar has melted, about 2 to 3 minutes. Remove from heat; stir in bourbon. Cool slightly.

Makes about 1 cup

Chocolate Almond Torte

Rich and decadent, this luscious torte will please even the most discriminating chocolate lover.

1³/4 cups flour

1³/4 cups sugar

1¹/4 teaspoons baking soda

1/4 teaspoon baking powder

1 teaspoon salt

1¹/4 cups water

²/3 cup butter or margarine, softened

4 squares (1 ounce each)
   unsweetened chocolate, melted
   and cooled

1/4 teaspoon almond extract

3 eggs

Chocolate Almond Frosting
   (recipe follows)

1/2 cup slivered almonds, toasted
   and chopped

In large mixer bowl, combine flour, sugar, baking soda, baking powder, and salt. Add water, butter, melted chocolate, and almond extract; beat at low speed until moistened. Beat at medium speed for 2 minutes, scraping sides and bottom of bowl often. Add eggs; beat at medium speed for 2 minutes. Grease bottom and sides of three 9-inch round cake pans. Divide batter evenly among pans; spread to smooth tops. Bake in 350°F oven until wooden pick inserted in center comes out clean, about 20 to 25 minutes. Cool in pans for 10 minutes. Invert cakes onto wire racks and cool completely.

TO ASSEMBLE Place one cake layer on serving plate. Spread top with 1/3 of the frosting. Stack remaining layers on top, spreading tops with frosting. Sprinkle almonds over top. Chill.

Makes 12 servings

Chocolate Almond Frosting

1 package (8 ounces) cream
   cheese, softened

1/4 cup butter, softened

3/4 cup powdered sugar

1 tablespoon unsweetened
   cocoa powder

1/4 cup almond-flavored liqueur
   (Amaretto)

In mixer bowl, beat cream cheese and butter at medium speed until light and fluffy. In small bowl, whisk together powdered sugar and cocoa. With mixer at low speed, gradually beat into cream cheese mixture. Beat in liqueur until smooth.

Makes enough to frost tops of three 9-inch layers

contributed by

Jeannie Rader

Home Economist Jeannie Rader brings with her a wealth of culinary experience. Jeannie retired after managing the West Oak School of Cooking for 22 years. She has shared her creative ideas, knowledge of cooking, and wonderful recipes in hundreds of classes for children, adults, and couples. While some of Jeannie's favorite classes focused on delectable entrées designed for stylish entertaining, you can be sure that dessert will always be something chocolate!

Per serving with frosting

Calories 517

Fat 31 g

Cholesterol 113 mg

Sodium 515 mg

Carbohydrate 57 g

Fiber 3 g

Lemon Lover's Cheesecake

This luscious cheesecake is a slice of heaven! Prepared lemon curd is an easy topping that adds a burst of lemon flavor.

CRUST
1 1/3 cups shortbread cookie crumbs
3 tablespoons butter, melted

FILLING
3 packages (8 ounces each) cream
    cheese, softened
3 tablespoons fresh lemon juice
1 cup sugar
1 tablespoon cornstarch
1 tablespoon grated lemon peel
3 eggs

TOPPING
1 jar (10 to 12 ounces) lemon curd
Whipped cream, raspberries, and
    mint sprigs

FOR CRUST In medium bowl, combine shortbread crumbs and butter until evenly moistened. Firmly press mixture into bottom of 9-inch springform pan that has been coated with no-stick cooking spray. Wrap foil under bottom and around outside of pan. Bake in 325°F oven for 8 minutes; set aside.

FOR FILLING In large mixer bowl, beat cream cheese at high speed until smooth. Beat in lemon juice. In small bowl, combine sugar, cornstarch, and lemon peel. Add to cream cheese mixture and beat until well mixed, scraping bowl occasionally. Add eggs, 1 at a time, beating at low speed after each addition just until blended. Pour filling into prepared crust. Bake in 325°F oven until edges are set and center is almost set, about 40 to 45 minutes. Turn off the oven. Loosen edges of cake from pan with sharp knife. Leave cheesecake in oven with door ajar for 30 minutes. Remove from oven. Cool on wire rack to room temperature. Cover and chill for 8 hours or overnight.

FOR TOPPING Spread lemon curd over cheesecake. Chill before removing springform ring. Just before serving, add dollop of whipped cream, fresh raspberries, and mint sprigs.

Makes 12 servings

TIP To cut cheesecake, use long, thin knife, wiping blade and dipping in hot water between cuts.

Lemon Curd

Lemon curd is a sweet, yet tart, spreadable cooked cream. It is different from a filling or custard because it contains more lemon juice and zest, giving it a brighter flavor. Butter gives it a smooth, velvety texture. Originating in England, lemon curd is traditionally served with scones at afternoon tea. It's also fabulous as a filling in trifles, tarts, and cakes.

Per serving

Calories 481
Fat 38 g
Cholesterol 132 mg
Sodium 280 mg
Carbohydrate 51 g
Fiber <1 g

185

Cranberry Swirl Cheesecake

We've swirled tart red cranberries into the richest filling for a truly extraordinary dessert. Garnish dessert plates with mint leaves and fresh cranberries for a festive touch.

ingredient savvy

Cranberries

Fresh cranberries are easy to freeze! Simply place the unopened package of berries in the freezer. When ready to use, rinse, drain, and add them frozen to cooked sauces. For baked goods, thaw in a colander before adding to batter. Fresh cranberries may be kept for up to two months in the refrigerator and for up to twelve months in the freezer.

CRANBERRY PURÉE

2 cups fresh or frozen cranberries

1 cup water

1/2 cup sugar

CHEESECAKE

1 cup chocolate wafer cookie crumbs

3 tablespoons butter or margarine, melted

4 packages (8 ounces each) cream cheese, softened

1 3/4 cups sugar

4 eggs, at room temperature

FOR PURÉE Place cranberries, water, and sugar in large saucepan; bring to a boil over medium-high heat. Reduce heat and simmer stirring occasionally until berries pop, about 5 minutes. Remove from heat and cool slightly. Place berries and their liquid in work bowl of food processor fitted with steel knife blade; process until puréed. Strain sauce through medium strainer; discard pulp.

FOR CHEESECAKE Wrap foil under bottom and around outside of 9-inch springform pan. In medium bowl, stir together cookie crumbs and butter until evenly moistened. Press into bottom of prepared pan. In large mixer bowl, beat cream cheese and sugar at high speed until smooth. Add eggs, 1 at a time, beating at low speed after each addition just until blended. Pour 1/3 of the batter over crust. Drizzle 1/4 cup purée over batter. Repeat batter and purée layers; top with remaining batter, smoothing gently. Drizzle 1 tablespoon purée over top. With knife, gently swirl through batter to marbleize. Place cheesecake in shallow pan. Pour water around cheesecake to come halfway up sides of springform pan. Bake in 350°F oven until edges are set and center is just slightly jiggly, about 60 to 65 minutes. Turn off the oven. Loosen edges of cake from pan with sharp knife. Leave cheesecake in oven with door ajar for 30 minutes. Remove from oven. Cool on wire rack to room temperature. Cover and chill overnight before removing springform ring. Serve with remaining cranberry purée.

Makes 10-12 servings

Per serving with purée

Calories 491

Fat 32 g

Cholesterol 162 mg

Sodium 327 mg

Carbohydrate 44 g

Fiber 1 g

Eggnog Pound Cake

A hint of nutmeg and a splash of rum add rich holiday flavor to this classic cake.
It's perfect for brunch or dessert.

1 cup butter or margarine, softened
2¾ cups granulated sugar
6 eggs
3 cups flour
¹/₂ teaspoon salt
¹/₄ teaspoon baking soda
1 cup dairy sour cream
¹/₄ cup light rum
¹/₂ teaspoon ground nutmeg
Rum Glaze (recipe follows)

In large mixer bowl, beat butter and sugar at medium speed until light and fluffy. Add eggs, 2 at a time, beating thoroughly after each addition. In medium bowl, whisk together flour, salt, and baking soda. In small bowl, combine sour cream, rum, and nutmeg. With mixer at low speed, add ¹/₄ of flour mixture to butter mixture alternately with ¹/₃ of the sour cream mixture (beginning and ending with flour mixture), beating after each addition. Pour batter into lightly greased 10-inch Bundt or tube pan. Bake in 350°F oven until wooden pick inserted in center comes out clean, about 65 to 70 minutes. Cool in pan for 10 minutes. Invert onto wire rack. Place over waxed paper. Drizzle Rum Glaze over warm cake.

Makes 16 servings

Rum Glaze

¹/₃ cup butter
2 cups powdered sugar
2 tablespoons light rum
¹/₈ teaspoon ground nutmeg
1 to 1¹/₂ tablespoons hot water

Place butter in 4-cup glass measure. Microwave (high) for 45 seconds or until melted. Stir in powdered sugar, rum, and nutmeg. Stir in water to desired consistency.

Makes ³/₄ cup

TIP If desired, substitute milk for rum in cake and glaze; add 2 teaspoons vanilla extract to cake, and 1 teaspoon vanilla extract to glaze.

technique savvy

Baking Hints

Baking is an exact art. These tips will ensure perfect baked goods.

Allow at least ten minutes for the oven to preheat.

Follow measuring and baking directions exactly as written.

Prepare cake pans prior to mixing the batter.

Cool cakes in their pans as directed on the package or in the recipe. Turn out onto a wire rack and allow to cool completely before frosting.

Per serving with glaze

Calories 480
Fat 21 g
Cholesterol 128 mg
Sodium 241 mg
Carbohydrate 67 g
Fiber 1 g

Swedish Spice Cake

Crystallized Ginger

Crystallized ginger, made from young slices of ginger root, is candied—or crystallized—by cooking it in sugar syrup, allowing it to dry, and coating it with sugar. It is most often used in dessert recipes. Try adding crystallized ginger to cookie dough, or waffle or pancake batters. Mix it into ice cream or stir-fries for a touch of spicy-sweet flavor.

Layer after moist, tender layer is spiced with crystallized ginger and a whisper of lemon.

1 tablespoon butter, softened
Slivered blanched almonds
1 box (18.25 ounces) yellow cake mix
4 eggs
1/3 cup water
1/3 cup dairy sour cream
1/4 cup finely chopped crystallized ginger
1 teaspoon grated lemon peel
1 1/2 teaspoons ground cinnamon
1/2 teaspoon ground nutmeg
Spiced Cream Cheese Filling (recipe follows)

Generously coat bottom and sides of one 9-inch round cake pan with softened butter. Use almond slivers to create several snowflake-type patterns on bottom of pan, grouping 6 almonds together. Chill about 10 minutes. Lightly coat second 9-inch round cake pan with no-stick cooking spray; set aside.

In large mixer bowl, combine cake mix, eggs, water, and sour cream. Beat at low speed just until combined. Add crystallized ginger, lemon peel, cinnamon, and nutmeg; beat at medium speed for 2 minutes. Divide cake batter between prepared pans. Bake in 350°F oven until wooden pick inserted in center comes out clean, about 20 to 22 minutes. Cool in pans for 10 minutes. Invert onto wire racks; cool completely. Split each cooled cake into 2 layers. Spread filling on tops only of the three plain layers. Carefully stack cakes together on serving plate. Place almond-decorated layer on top. Chill until ready to serve.

Makes 12 servings

Spiced Cream Cheese Filling

2 packages (8 ounces each) cream cheese, softened
1/2 cup dairy sour cream
1 cup powdered sugar
1/4 cup finely chopped crystallized ginger
1 teaspoon vanilla extract
1/2 teaspoon ground cinnamon

In large mixer bowl, beat cream cheese at medium speed until fluffy. Beat in sour cream. Add powdered sugar, crystallized ginger, vanilla, and cinnamon; beat at low speed until blended. Beat at medium speed until fluffy.

Makes 3 cups

Per serving with filling

Calories 444
Fat 24 g
Cholesterol 122 mg
Sodium 440 mg
Carbohydrate 51 g
Fiber 1 g

Pineapple Carrot Cake

Studded with pineapple and pecans, this lighter-textured carrot cake is a great take-along for barbecues, picnics, or anytime you need to bring dessert. The spiced cream cheese frosting is the crowning touch.

Cream Cheese

It's often tempting to use a lower-fat or fat-free variety of cream cheese to reduce calories and fat. Unfortunately, not all cream cheese is created equal, and substituting can affect the finished product. Using a reduced-fat cream cheese can result in cake frostings that slide right off the cake, and cheese balls and cheesecakes that never set up. For best results, use regular cream cheese unless the recipe specifies that a reduced-fat variety will work.

Per serving with frosting

Calories 452
Fat 25 g
Cholesterol 109 mg
Sodium 247 mg
Carbohydrate 54 g
Fiber 1 g

1 package (18.25 ounces) spice cake mix
1 package (4-serving size) instant vanilla pudding mix
1 can (8 ounces) crushed pineapple in juice
1/3 cup vegetable oil
1/4 cup water
4 eggs
2 cups shredded carrots (about 8 ounces)
1 cup chopped pecans (divided)
Cinnamon Cream Cheese Frosting (recipe follows)

In large mixer bowl, combine cake mix, pudding mix, pineapple with juice, oil, water, and eggs; beat at low speed for 30 seconds until blended. Beat at medium speed for 1 1/2 minutes. Fold in carrots and 1/2 cup of the pecans. Spread batter in 9×13-inch baking pan that has been coated with no-stick cooking spray. Bake in 350°F oven until wooden pick inserted in center comes out clean, about 40 to 45 minutes. Cool completely in pan on wire rack. Spread frosting over top. Sprinkle with remaining 1/2 cup pecans. Refrigerate several hours before serving to set frosting.

Makes 12-16 servings

Cinnamon Cream Cheese Frosting

1 package (8 ounces) cream cheese, softened
4 tablespoons butter, softened
3 cups powdered sugar
1 teaspoon vanilla extract
1/2 teaspoon ground cinnamon

In large mixer bowl, beat cream cheese and butter at medium speed until creamy. Add powdered sugar, vanilla, and cinnamon. Beat at low speed just until smooth. Spread on cooled cake immediately.

Makes frosting for top of 9×13-inch cake

TIP Do not substitute reduced-fat or whipped cream cheese in frosting recipe.

Ultimate Fudge Cake

This deep, dark, and decadent cake was designed with chocolate lovers in mind.
It's the perfect finale to any occasion.

1 package (18.25 ounces) devil's
    food cake mix
1 cup semi-sweet chocolate chunks
1 bar (4 ounces) bittersweet
    chocolate, broken
3 tablespoons milk
2 tablespoons butter
1/2 cup powdered sugar
Mini chocolate chips or chopped nuts

Prepare cake batter according to package directions; stir in chocolate chunks. Bake in Bundt pan according to package directions. Cool in pan for 10 minutes. Invert onto wire rack; cool completely.

FOR GLAZE In 1-quart glass bowl, combine bittersweet chocolate, milk, and butter. Microwave (high) for 1 minute. Whisk in powdered sugar until smooth. Drizzle over cake. Garnish with mini chocolate chips or nuts.

Makes 16 servings

TIP For the holidays, add 1 teaspoon peppermint extract to batter and garnish top with crushed peppermint candies.

Chocolate Bloom

Store chocolate tightly wrapped in a cool (60° to 70°F) place, away from strong-flavored foods. Warm temperatures can cause the cocoa butter to rise to the surface of the chocolate, creating a pale gray coloration called "bloom." The bloom is harmless and has little or no effect on flavor or texture.

Per serving

Calories 352
Fat 19 g
Cholesterol 46 mg
Sodium 283 mg
Carbohydrate 42 g
Fiber 2 g

Jumbleberry Trifle

Layer luscious lemon cream, ribbon-striped pound cake, and a tart berry sauce in stemmed glasses for an elegant take on a classic dessert.

contributed by

Cathy Chipley

Former Staff Home Economist and School of Cooking Manager, Cathy Chipley has a wealth of knowledge about food. She is also a Registered Dietitian and co-host of *Dierbergs Presents Everybody Cooks®* television show. While living in Europe, Cathy taught English as a second language. She has a fresh, hands-on approach to cooking. Baking is her specialty and she does it with ease—everything from rich and decadent desserts to simple everyday treats.

1 bag (12 ounces) frozen unsweetened raspberries, thawed
1 jar (12 ounces) seedless blackberry jam (divided)
1 box (10.75 ounces) frozen pound cake, thawed
2 tablespoons cream sherry or almond-flavored liqueur (Amaretto)
1 jar (10 to 12 ounces) lemon curd
2 cups heavy whipping cream
Fresh berries and mint

In medium bowl, combine raspberries with 1 cup of the jam. Use back of spoon to strain mixture through fine sieve; discard seeds. Chill. Cut pound cake into 1/2-inch thick slices. Split each piece into 1/4-inch thick slices. Spread some of the remaining jam over half of the slices. Place plain slices on top of jam and sandwich pieces together; cut into 1/2-inch cubes. Brush sherry over cubes; set aside. In large mixer bowl, beat lemon curd and whipping cream at low speed until blended. Beat at high speed until soft peaks form; chill.

To ASSEMBLE Spoon 2 tablespoons berry sauce into bottom of 8 large wine or parfait glasses. Top each with 1/4 cup cake cubes. Add 1/4 cup lemon cream mixture. Repeat layers. Chill until ready to serve. If desired, garnish with fresh berries and mint.

Makes 8 servings

Per serving

Calories 614
Fat 41 g
Cholesterol 131 mg
Sodium 195 mg
Carbohydrate 78 g
Fiber 1 g

Very Berry Chocolate Chip Pie

Put all of your favorite flavors into one very pretty pie? Why not! A simple cookie crust, plump, juicy strawberries, and a drizzle of chocolate are too tempting to resist.

ingredient savvy

Fresh Strawberries

Fresh strawberries need a little TLC. Store unwashed berries loosely covered in the refrigerator for up to two or three days. Don't store them in a plastic bag or allow them to sit in water, as they will lose color and flavor, and get soft spots. Just before using, place berries in a colander and rinse under cold running water. Drain on paper towels and remove the stems and caps.

1 roll (18 ounces) refrigerated
    chocolate chip cookie dough
1 package (8 ounces) cream
    cheese, softened
1/4 cup sugar
1 teaspoon vanilla extract
1 pound strawberries
    (about 20 to 25 medium berries)
1/4 cup semi-sweet chocolate chips

Slice cookie dough; pat evenly into 9-inch pie plate that has been coated with no-stick cooking spray. Bake in 350°F oven until center is set, about 20 to 22 minutes; cool completely on wire rack. In medium bowl, beat cream cheese, sugar, and vanilla with hand mixer at medium speed until smooth. Cover and chill.

Just before serving, spread cream cheese mixture over cooled crust. Rinse berries; dry thoroughly on paper towels. Remove caps and stems. Arrange berries upright on top of cream cheese layer, covering entire surface. Place chocolate chips in small freezer-weight reclosable plastic bag; seal bag. Immerse bag in bowl of very hot water until melted; wipe bag dry. Knead chocolate in bag until completely smooth. Snip off one corner of bag to make small hole. Drizzle chocolate over tops of berries. Serve immediately.

Makes 8 servings

TIP For best appearance, select berries that are similar in size.

Per serving

Calories 449
Fat 25 g
Cholesterol 47 mg
Sodium 218 mg
Carbohydrate 54 g
Fiber 2 g

Baked Alaska Pie

Crispy on the outside, gooey on the inside! A quick marshmallow topping crowns this fun-to-serve dessert.

1¹/₃ cups chocolate cookie crumbs
¹/₄ cup sugar
¹/₄ cup butter, melted
¹/₂ cup seedless raspberry jam
4 cups (1 quart) chocolate chip
    ice cream
1 jar (7 ounces) marshmallow creme
2 cups miniature marshmallows

In medium bowl, mix cookie crumbs, sugar, and butter until evenly moistened. Firmly press into bottom and up sides of 9-inch metal pie pan. Freeze for 15 minutes. Spread raspberry jam over crust. Mound ice cream over jam, pressing and smoothing into crust. Cover with plastic wrap and freeze until very firm, at least 6 hours.

Remove lid and entire seal from marshmallow creme jar. Microwave (high) for 20 seconds to soften. Spread over pie, completely covering ice cream. Sprinkle marshmallows in single layer over creme. Place pie pan on foil-lined baking sheet. Bake in 475°F oven until marshmallows are lightly browned, about 2 to 3 minutes. Use wet knife to cut into wedges; serve immediately. Store leftover pie in freezer.

Makes 8-10 servings

TIP To brown marshmallows without melting ice cream, be sure oven is preheated to 475°F.

Baked Alaska

Baked Alaska was served as far back as the early 1800s when Thomas Jefferson served it to his dinner guests at the White House. Time has changed the recipe, but not the process.

The key to a successful Baked Alaska is ensuring the ice cream is frozen solid and that the oven is very hot. Be sure the marshmallow creme or meringue completely covers the ice cream and protects it from the heat. Yes—it really works!

Per serving

Calories 411
Fat 14 g
Cholesterol 34 mg
Sodium 211 mg
Carbohydrate 67 g
Fiber 1 g

Roasted Pear Tart

Roasting the pears makes them delectably sweet and tender. A drizzle of hazelnut liqueur adds a wonderful flavor to the filling.

3 pears, each cut into 8 wedges
    (Bosc, Anjou, or Bartlett)
1 tablespoon granulated sugar
1 tablespoon lemon juice
1/4 teaspoon ground cinnamon

CRUST
6 large, soft oatmeal cookies
1/4 cup plain dry bread crumbs
1 egg white, slightly beaten

FILLING
1 package (8 ounces) cream
    cheese, softened
2 tablespoons brown sugar
2 tablespoons hazelnut or almond-
    flavored liqueur (Frangelico,
    Amaretto)
1 cup heavy whipping cream,
    whipped, or 1 container
    (8 ounces) fat free frozen
    non-dairy whipped topping,
    thawed

Place pear wedges in jellyroll pan. In small bowl, combine granulated sugar, lemon juice, and cinnamon. Drizzle over pears, tossing to coat. Spread pears in single layer. Roast in 400°F oven for 20 minutes, turning pears over halfway through cooking time. Cool completely.

FOR CRUST In work bowl of food processor fitted with steel knife blade, process cookies until finely chopped. Add bread crumbs and egg white; pulse until evenly mixed. Press mixture onto bottom and 1/4-inch up sides of lightly greased 9-inch tart pan with removable bottom. Bake in 400°F oven until lightly browned, about 5 minutes. Cool completely.

FOR FILLING In large mixer bowl, beat cream cheese, brown sugar, and liqueur at medium speed until smooth. Fold in whipped cream. Spread filling in cooled crust. Arrange roasted pears over top.

Makes 8 servings

TIP If desired, light cream cheese may be used in this recipe.

Per serving with light cream cheese and fat-free whipped topping

Calories 272
Fat 8 g
Cholesterol 19 mg
Sodium 208 mg
Carbohydrate 43 g
Fiber 2 g

contributed by

Loretta Evans

Staff Home Economist Loretta Evans has been a Dierbergs School of Cooking Manager since 1997. While growing up in Southern Illinois, Loretta enjoyed spending time in the kitchen with her grandmother. She earned a degree in Dietetics, and worked as a food technologist before completing a culinary arts program. Students love Loretta's down-to-earth approach to cooking and wonderful sense of humor in her classes on baking, desserts, and lighter-style cooking.

Per serving

Calories 361
Fat 24 g
Cholesterol 75 mg
Sodium 207 mg
Carbohydrate 33 g
Fiber 2 g

Chocolate Pecan Pie Bars

Two favorite holiday pies combine in these tempting take-along bars.

technique savvy

Cutting Perfect Bars

Creating perfectly cut bar cookies is easy! Line a baking pan with heavy-duty foil, allowing it to extend over the edge of the pan. Bake and cool as directed. Use the foil to lift baked bar cookies from the pan. Place them on a cutting board and use a large sharp knife to cut straight down through the bars for neat, even cuts.

CRUST

1 1/2 cups flour

1/4 cup butter, softened

1/4 cup firmly packed brown sugar

1/2 teaspoon salt

1/2 cup semi-sweet chocolate chips

FILLING

4 eggs

1 cup light corn syrup

1/3 cup firmly packed brown sugar

1/4 cup butter, melted

3 tablespoons flour

1 teaspoon vanilla extract

2 cups coarsely chopped pecans

FOR CRUST Line 9×13-inch baking pan with foil or parchment paper, extending about 1 inch above sides of pan. In large mixer bowl, beat flour, butter, brown sugar, and salt at medium speed until crumbs form. Press into bottom of prepared pan. Bake in 350°F oven until light brown and set, about 15 minutes. Remove from oven. Sprinkle chocolate chips over crust; let stand 5 minutes. Spread chocolate evenly over crust.

FOR FILLING In large mixer bowl, beat eggs at high speed until thick and lemon colored, about 2 to 3 minutes. Stir in corn syrup, brown sugar, butter, flour, and vanilla until smooth. Fold in pecans. Pour filling over crust. Bake in 350°F oven until knife inserted in center comes out clean, about 25 to 30 minutes. Cool completely in pan on wire rack. Use edges of foil to lift from pan onto cutting board. Cut into bars. Store tightly covered in refrigerator.

Makes 48 bars

TIP One roll (18 ounces) refrigerated sugar cookie dough can be sliced and pressed evenly into pan to form crust. Bake and proceed as directed.

Per bar

Calories 110

Fat 6 g

Cholesterol 23 mg

Sodium 54 mg

Carbohydrate 13 g

Fiber 1 g

Gooey Butter Brownie Bars

The famous St. Louis gooey butter topping meets a rich chocolate brownie base to create these fabulous two-layer bars. They're rich, decadent, and worth every bite!

BROWNIE BASE

2 squares (1 ounce each)
    unsweetened chocolate

1/3 cup butter or margarine

1 cup sugar

2 eggs

1 teaspoon vanilla extract

1/2 cup flour

GOOEY BUTTER TOPPING

2/3 cup sugar

1/4 cup butter or margarine, softened

1 egg

1/4 cup milk

1/4 cup light corn syrup

1 teaspoon vanilla extract

1/2 cup flour

Dash salt

Powdered sugar

FOR BASE In large microwave-safe bowl, combine chocolate and butter. Microwave (high) for 1 1/2 to 2 minutes. Stir until chocolate is melted and smooth. Stir in sugar. Stir in eggs and vanilla until well blended. Stir in flour. Spread into 8-inch square pan that has been lined with foil and coated with no-stick cooking spray. Bake in 350°F oven for 20 minutes.

FOR TOPPING In large mixer bowl, beat sugar and butter at medium speed until light and fluffy. Beat in egg. Gradually beat in milk, corn syrup, and vanilla. With mixer at low speed, beat in flour and salt until well combined. Pour over partially baked brownie base. Bake in 350°F oven until light golden brown and center of topping is set, about 17 to 20 minutes. Cool completely in pan on wire rack. Sprinkle powdered sugar over top. Use edges of foil to lift from pan onto cutting board. Cut into bars.

Makes 24 bars

Gooey Butter Cake

Gooey Butter Cake is a St. Louis tradition that was created quite by accident. The legend says that in the 1930s, a St. Louis baker incorrectly measured ingredients for a traditional butter cake. What came out of the oven was a buttery coffee cake base with a gooey rich topping. That delicious "mistake" has been a favorite treat ever since!

Per bar

Calories 145

Fat 7 g

Cholesterol 39 mg

Sodium 54 mg

Carbohydrate 21 g

Fiber 1 g

kid approved recipes

Kids in the Kitchen

Dips and Dunkers

Take a break from fast food and stock the fridge with good food that's fast! Creamy, dreamy dips and fresh fruit and veggie dunkers are tasty anytime.

Sunshine Fruit Dip

1 carton (16 ounces) low-fat vanilla yogurt
1 package (4-serving size) instant vanilla pudding
1/2 cup milk
2 teaspoons grated orange peel

Place all ingredients in medium bowl. Whisk until well blended. Cover and refrigerate for up to 5 days. Serve with assorted fresh fruit.

Makes 2 1/2 cups

Almond Cream Dip

1 package (8 ounces) light cream cheese, softened
3 tablespoons powdered sugar
3 tablespoons light dairy sour cream
1/4 teaspoon almond extract

In small bowl, beat cream cheese with hand mixer until fluffy. Beat in remaining ingredients until thoroughly blended. Cover and refrigerate for up to 3 days. Serve with assorted fresh fruit.

Makes 1 1/4 cups

Silly Dilly Dip

1 cup (8 ounces) light dairy sour cream
2/3 cup low-fat mayonnaise
1 tablespoon dried parsley flakes
1 teaspoon dried dill weed
1/2 teaspoon onion powder

In medium mixing bowl, combine sour cream and mayonnaise; stir until well blended. Stir in parsley, dill, and onion powder. Cover and refrigerate for up to 5 days. Serve with assorted vegetable dippers.

Makes 1 2/3 cups

Zesty Taco Dip

1 package (8 ounces) light cream
    cheese, softened
1 cup (8 ounces) light dairy sour
    cream
1 envelope (1.25 ounces) taco
    seasoning mix
1 Roma tomato, chopped
1/2 cup thinly sliced green onion

In medium bowl, stir together cream cheese, sour cream, and taco seasoning until well blended. Stir in tomato and green onion. Cover and refrigerate for 3 to 4 hours or overnight to allow flavors to blend. Serve with assorted vegetable dippers.

Makes 2 1/2 cups

Per 2 tablespoons

Calories 48
Fat 3 g
Cholesterol 10 mg
Sodium 209 mg
Carbohydrate 4 g
Fiber <1 g

Strawberry Banana Smoothie

This creamy shake is cool, frosty, and berry-licious!

2 cups fresh strawberries, rinsed
    and hulls removed
2 ripe bananas, cut into chunks
1 cup vanilla frozen yogurt or
    ice cream
1 cup milk

Place all ingredients in blender container or in work bowl of food processor fitted with steel knife blade. Blend until smooth. Serve immediately.

Makes 3 servings

TIP When you make smoothies, be sure that all ingredients are cold. If you start with frozen fruit, the smoothie will be thick—just like a shake.

Per serving

Calories 235
Fat 5 g
Cholesterol 17 mg
Sodium 70 mg
Carbohydrate 43 g
Fiber 4 g

**Per serving with
fat-free frozen yogurt and
nonfat milk**

Calories 189
Fat 1 g
Cholesterol 2 mg
Sodium 68 mg
Carbohydrate 42 g
Fiber 4 g

That's Italian Salad

Everybody loves this salad. It tastes just like the one you get at your favorite Italian restaurant. Now you can make it yourself!

junior chef hints

Chilly Greens

Rinse bagged salad greens, drain well, and roll in paper towels. Refrigerate for about an hour before serving so they will be cold and crisp for your salad.

1 head iceberg lettuce
1 head romaine lettuce
1 can (14 ounces) artichoke hearts in water, drained and coarsely chopped
1/2 cup very thinly sliced red onion
1/4 cup grated parmesan cheese
Classic Italian Dressing (recipe follows)

Rinse lettuce and tear into bite-sized pieces. Pat with paper towels or spin dry. Place in large salad bowl. Add remaining ingredients except dressing. Cover and chill several hours to crisp lettuce. When ready to serve, shake dressing until well combined. Drizzle over salad and toss to coat.

Makes 8 servings

Classic Italian Dressing

6 tablespoons vegetable or olive oil
1/4 cup red wine vinegar
2 tablespoons chopped pimientos (optional)
2 tablespoons grated parmesan cheese
1 tablespoon sugar
1/4 teaspoon salt
1/4 teaspoon pepper

Combine all ingredients in 1 or 2-cup container with tight-fitting lid. Shake until well blended. If desired, cover and chill several hours or overnight.

Makes 3/4 cup

Per serving with dressing

Calories 136
Fat 11 g
Cholesterol 1 mg
Sodium 311 mg
Carbohydrate 9 g
Fiber 2 g

Wrap and Roll Sandwiches

Who needs bread to make a sandwich? Roll up your favorite fillings in a soft tortilla for a neat sandwich that's really delicious.

1 package (8 ounces) light cream
   cheese, softened
$1/4$ cup light ranch dressing
8 large flour tortillas
   (8-inch diameter)
$1/2$ pound sliced turkey
$1/2$ pound sliced ham
2 cups shredded lettuce

In medium bowl with hand mixer, beat together cream cheese and dressing. Stack tortillas between damp paper towels. Microwave (high) for 30 seconds or according to package directions. Spread a generous tablespoon of the cream cheese mixture on each tortilla. Place one or two slices each of turkey and ham in center of each tortilla. Sprinkle shredded lettuce over top. Fold in about 1 inch on one side of each tortilla, then roll tightly to enclose filling.

Makes 8 wraps

MAKE-AHEAD TIP Wrap each sandwich in foil or plastic wrap and refrigerate for several hours before serving.

junior chef hints

Tortilla Wraps

Corn tortillas are more firm than flour tortillas and are fried to make taco shells and chips. Flour tortillas are softer and great for making burritos. They also come in different colors and are fun to wrap around sandwich fillings.

Per wrap

Calories 314
Fat 15 g
Cholesterol 58 mg
Sodium 1082 mg
Carbohydrate 26 g
Fiber 1 g

Pizza Pull-Aparts

You've never had pizza like this before! Let these gooey pizza spirals bake together so you can pull them apart.

1 recipe Super Simple Pizza Crust
    dough (recipe on page 130)
1 teaspoon Italian herb seasoning
1 can (6 ounces) tomato paste
2/3 cup shredded mozzarella cheese
2/3 cup chopped pepperoni
1/4 cup grated parmesan cheese

Lightly coat 9-inch round cake pan with no-stick cooking spray; set aside. On lightly floured surface, roll dough into 8×12-inch rectangle. In small bowl, stir Italian seasoning into tomato paste; spread over dough. Sprinkle remaining ingredients over top. Roll up jellyroll fashion, beginning at one long end. Moisten edges with water and pinch together to seal firmly. Using thin string or dental floss, slice roll into 12 pieces. Place pizza rolls, cut-side up, in prepared pan; cover and let rise for 30 minutes.

Preheat oven to 375°F. Bake until golden brown, about 20 to 25 minutes. Cool in pan for 5 minutes. Serve warm.

Makes 12 rolls

Temperature Zone

Use a thermometer to check the water temperature when making yeast dough. If it's too cold, the yeast won't grow, and if it's too hot, the dough won't rise.

Per roll

Calories 159
Fat 6 g
Cholesterol 13 mg
Sodium 404 mg
Carbohydrate 20 g
Fiber 2 g

Mama Mia Mostaccioli

Because of the shape of the noodles, this pasta was named "mostaccioli," which means mustache in Italian. In English, we think it means "delicious."

1 box (16 ounces) mostaccioli noodles
1 pound lean ground beef
1 can (48 ounces) tomato juice
1 can (6 ounces) tomato paste
1/2 medium onion, chopped
1/4 cup sugar
1/2 teaspoon garlic powder
1/2 teaspoon salt
1/4 teaspoon ground black pepper
Grated parmesan cheese

In large pot of boiling water, cook mostaccioli noodles according to package directions; drain well. While noodles cook, crumble ground beef into preheated large saucepan. Cook over medium-high heat, stirring occasionally, until browned. Drain off any fat. Add remaining ingredients except cheese; bring to a boil. Reduce heat and simmer for 15 minutes. Stir drained pasta into sauce until well mixed. Serve with parmesan cheese.

Makes 8 servings

Per serving without parmesan

Calories 372
Fat 5 g
Cholesterol 33 mg
Sodium 845 mg
Carbohydrate 61 g
Fiber 3 g

Chinese Fried Rice

Create a Chinese restaurant right in your own kitchen. This fried rice is even better than your favorite take-out.

2 tablespoons vegetable oil (divided)
1 cup shredded carrot
1/2 cup thinly sliced green onion
1/2 cup frozen peas, thawed
1 teaspoon grated fresh ginger root
2 cups cooked rice, chilled
2 eggs, slightly beaten
1 tablespoon soy sauce

In wok or large skillet, heat 1 tablespoon of the oil over medium-high heat. Add carrot, green onion, peas, and ginger; stir-fry for 1 minute. Push vegetables to sides of wok. Add remaining 1 tablespoon oil to center of wok. Add rice; stir-fry for 2 to 3 minutes. Push rice to sides of wok. Add eggs to center of wok; cook, stirring constantly until eggs are scrambled and set. Stir rice and vegetables into scrambled eggs. Sprinkle soy sauce over rice. Stir-fry until well mixed and heated through.

Makes 2-4 servings

No Gummy Fried Rice!

To keep the fried rice from getting gummy, start with cold, cooked rice. It will cool faster if you spread the cooked rice in a baking pan and put it in the refrigerator.

Per serving

Calories 231
Fat 10 g
Cholesterol 106 mg
Sodium 307 mg
Carbohydrate 29 g
Fiber 2 g

P B & J Bubble Ring

Two favorites—peanut butter and jelly—make this hot, flaky loaf a breakfast treat.

Baker's Golden Rule

Always preheat the oven for ten minutes before you bake anything. This makes sure that the oven has reached the correct temperature before you put the food in.

1/2 cup jelly or preserves (any flavor)

1/4 cup crunchy peanut butter

2 tablespoons butter or margarine

2 tablespoons honey

2 cans (7.5 ounces each) refrigerated biscuits

Preheat oven to 350°F. Coat Bundt pan or 6 1/2-cup ring mold with no-stick cooking spray; set aside.

Place jelly in 1-cup glass measure. Microwave (high) for 1 minute or until jelly melts; set aside. In second 1-cup glass measure, combine peanut butter, butter, and honey. Microwave (high) for 1 minute or until butter melts. Stir until mixture is smooth.

Separate each can of biscuit dough into 10 biscuits. Use scissors to cut each biscuit into 4 pieces. Place half of the biscuit pieces in bottom of prepared pan. Drizzle half of the melted jelly and half of the peanut butter mixture over biscuits. Top with remaining biscuit pieces; drizzle with remaining jelly and peanut butter mixture.

Bake in 350°F oven until golden brown, about 20 to 25 minutes. Carefully invert onto serving plate. Serve warm.

Makes 10 servings

Per serving

Calories 237

Fat 11 g

Cholesterol 7 mg

Sodium 496 mg

Carbohydrate 33 g

Fiber 1 g

Drumstick Ice Cream Pie

Some things you never outgrow! Packed with chocolate, peanuts, and ice cream, kids of all ages will love this frosty pie that tastes just like their favorite cone.

junior chef hints

No-Stick Trick

Here's a neat trick—coat the measuring cup lightly with no-stick cooking spray before measuring peanut butter. It will slide right out of the cup without a struggle, and cleanup will be a little easier.

2/3 cup chocolate fudge topping
2 tablespoons creamy peanut butter
One 9-inch pie shell, baked
1 quart vanilla ice cream, softened
2 tablespoons coarsely chopped
   peanuts

In small bowl, mix fudge topping with peanut butter until smooth. Spread half of the mixture in bottom of baked pie shell. Freeze 1 hour.

Spoon ice cream into pie shell, smoothing surface. Freeze 1 hour.

Drizzle remaining fudge mixture over ice cream, spreading to create marbled effect. Sprinkle peanuts over top. Cover and freeze until firm, at least 6 hours. Place pie in refrigerator for 10 to 15 minutes before serving for easier cutting.

Makes 8 servings

Per serving

Calories 377
Fat 19 g
Cholesterol 29 mg
Sodium 237 mg
Carbohydrate 46 g
Fiber 2 g

Old Glory Cookie Pizza

Three cheers for the red, white, and blueberries! This berry-covered cookie dessert is a flag-waving treat.

1 roll (18 ounces) refrigerated sugar cookie dough

2 cups (12 ounces) white baking chips (divided)

1 package (8 ounces) cream cheese, softened

1 container (8 ounces) frozen non-dairy whipped topping, thawed

1¼ cups blueberries

3¼ cups medium strawberries, rinsed, hulls removed, and quartered

Preheat oven to 350°F. Lightly coat 15×10-inch jellyroll pan with no-stick cooking spray. Slice cookie dough; place in single layer in prepared pan. Pat out dough to make even crust. Sprinkle 1 cup of the chips over crust; press lightly into dough. Bake in 350°F oven until golden brown, about 15 to 18 minutes; cool.

Place remaining 1 cup chips in medium microwave-safe bowl. Microwave (high) for 1 to 2 minutes, stirring once. Beat in cream cheese with hand mixer at high speed until smooth. Gently fold in whipped topping. Spread over cooled crust.

To make flag pattern, place blueberries in upper left corner for stars; arrange strawberries, cut-side down, in 7 rows for stripes. Chill at least 1 hour. Cut into bars or squares.

Makes 28 bars

Strawberry Cookie Pizza

Omit blueberries. Cut 14 strawberries in half. Arrange strawberry halves, cut-side down, in rows 7 across and 4 down. Place 1 cup of semi-sweet chocolate chips in small freezer-weight reclosable plastic bag; seal bag. Immerse bag in bowl of very hot water until chocolate melts; wipe bag dry. Knead chocolate through plastic until smooth. Snip off 1 corner of bag to make small hole. Drizzle melted chocolate over berries. Cut between berries into 28 bars.

junior chef hints

It's in the Bag

Wash hands and put a plastic bag over each hand. Pat cookie dough into the pan and the dough won't stick to your hands!

Per bar

Calories 209

Fat 12 g

Cholesterol 14 mg

Sodium 119 mg

Carbohydrate 23 g

Fiber 1 g

213

Candy Corn Cookies

Trick or treat, aren't these neat? These cookies sure are fun to eat. But you best beware! For if you blink, they'll disappear—quick as a wink!

The Scoop on Flour

Spoon flour lightly into nested measuring cups—not glass cups—and use a straight edge to sweep the excess off the top. This prevents flour from packing too tightly and making cookie dough too stiff.

3/4 cup (1 1/2 sticks) butter, softened
3/4 cup sugar
1 egg
1 1/2 teaspoons vanilla extract
2 1/4 cups flour
1/4 teaspoon baking powder
1/4 teaspoon salt
1/4 teaspoon yellow food color
1/4 teaspoon red food color

In large mixer bowl, beat together butter and sugar at medium speed until light and fluffy. Beat in egg and vanilla. In medium bowl, whisk together flour, baking powder, and salt. Add to butter mixture; beat at low speed just until combined. Remove 1/4 cup of the dough; set aside. Add yellow food color to remaining dough; mix until color is even. Remove 1 cup of the yellow dough; set aside. Add red food color to remaining dough in mixer bowl; mix until color is an even bright orange.

Cut 11x6-inch piece of medium-weight cardboard (empty cereal box works well). Fold in half lengthwise, sharply creasing fold. Cover cardboard with foil. Roll white dough into 11-inch strip. Hold cardboard in V shape; press white dough firmly into point of V. Roll orange dough in same manner and press on top of white dough in cardboard mold. Repeat with yellow dough, pressing on top of orange dough. Press firmly into cardboard mold. Wrap foil around cardboard mold to hold it in shape. Refrigerate at least 1 hour or until dough is very firm.

Preheat oven to 350°F. Remove cardboard mold. Use large knife to slice dough into 1/4-inch-thick triangles. Place on ungreased or parchment-lined baking sheets. Gently shape edges as needed to make candy corn shape. If dough becomes too soft to cut easily, refrigerate until firm. Bake in 350°F oven until set but not browned, about 10 minutes. Cool on wire racks.

Makes about 3 dozen cookies

Per cookie

Calories 82
Fat 4 g
Cholesterol 17 mg
Sodium 50 mg
Carbohydrate 10 g
Fiber <1 g

Caramel Corn Crunch

You and your friends will love this crispy, crunchy snack made with homemade caramel corn and your favorite candies. Watch how fast it disappears!

Pack It In!

Pack brown sugar firmly into nested measuring cups—not glass cups—and use a straight edge to scrape off the excess.

2 quarts (8 cups) popped corn

1 cup dry roasted peanuts

1/2 cup (1 stick) butter

2/3 cup firmly packed brown sugar

1 teaspoon vanilla extract

1/4 teaspoon salt

1 cup candy-coated chocolate pieces (M & M's, Reese's Pieces) or candy corn

Preheat oven to 350°F. Combine popcorn and peanuts in 9×13-inch pan. Combine butter, brown sugar, vanilla, and salt in 2-cup glass measure. Microwave (high) for 1 1/2 minutes; whisk until smooth and slightly thickened. Drizzle over popcorn mixture; stir until popcorn is evenly coated.

Bake in 350°F oven for 10 to 12 minutes, stirring twice during baking time, until coating is dry. Spread onto foil-lined tray to cool completely. Stir in candies. Store in airtight container.

Makes about 2 1/2 quarts

Per cup

Calories 305

Fat 21 g

Cholesterol 27 mg

Sodium 314 mg

Carbohydrate 27 g

Fiber 2 g

EQUIVALENTS

Pinch or dash	= Less than $1/8$ teaspoon
1 tablespoon	= 3 teaspoons
1 fluid ounce	= 2 tablespoons
$1/4$ cup	= 4 tablespoons
$1/3$ cup	= 5 tablespoons + 1 teaspoon
1 cup	= 16 tablespoons or 8 fluid ounces
1 cup	= $1/2$ pint
1 pint	= 2 cups or 16 fluid ounces
1 quart	= 2 pints or 32 fluid ounces
1 gallon	= 4 quarts
1 pound	= 16 ounces
1 cup soft bread crumbs	= 2 slices bread
4 ounces parmesan	= 1 cup grated
1 medium lemon	= 3 tablespoons juice, 2 to 3 teaspoons zest
1 medium lime	= $1^{1}/2$ to 2 tablespoons juice, 1 teaspoon zest
1 medium orange	= $1/3$ to $1/2$ cup juice, $1^{1}/2$ to 2 tablespoons zest
12 graham crackers	= 1 cup crushed
1 stick butter	= $1/2$ cup, $1/4$ pound, or 8 tablespoons
1 cup whipping cream	= 2 cups whipped cream
1 cup uncooked rice	= 3 cups cooked rice
1 pound granulated sugar	= $2^{1}/4$ cups
1 pound powdered sugar	= $3^{3}/4$ cups unsifted
1 pound brown sugar	= $2^{1}/2$ cups firmly packed
$1/4$ ounce envelope yeast	= $1/4$ teaspoon yeast

EMERGENCY SUBSTITUTIONS

For this ingredient	You may substitute
1 teaspoon baking powder	$1/4$ teaspoon baking soda + $1/2$ teaspoon cream of tartar
1 ounce (1 square) semi-sweet chocolate	$1/2$ ounce unsweetened chocolate + 1 tablespoon granulated sugar
6 ounces semi-sweet chocolate chips	Rounded $1/2$ cup unsweetened cocoa + $1/2$ cup granulated sugar + 3 tablespoons melted butter or margarine
1 ounce (1 square) unsweetened chocolate	3 tablespoons unsweetened cocoa + 1 tablespoon melted butter or margarine
1 cup buttermilk	1 tablespoon lemon juice or white vinegar + enough milk to equal 1 cup (let stand 5 minutes); or 1 cup plain yogurt
1 cup cake flour	1 cup minus 2 tablespoons sifted all-purpose flour
1 cup self-rising flour	1 cup all-purpose flour + $1^{1}/2$ teaspoons baking powder + $1/2$ teaspoon salt
1 tablespoon cornstarch (for thickening)	2 tablespoons all-purpose flour
1 tablespoon fresh herbs	1 teaspoon dried herbs; or $3/4$ teaspoon ground herbs
1 teaspoon pumpkin pie spice	$1/2$ teaspoon ground cinnamon + $1/2$ teaspoon ground ginger + $1/8$ teaspoon ground allspice + $1/8$ teaspoon ground nutmeg
1 cup dark corn syrup	$3/4$ cup light corn syrup + $1/4$ cup light molasses

INDEX